WALKER SUN BOOKS

SB- 1 *Islam* by Dominique Sourdel

SB- 2 *Africa Before the White Man* by Henri Labouret

SB- 3 *War* by Gaston Bouthoul

SB- 4 *Buddhism* by Henri Arvon

SB- 5 *The Nature of Hinduism* by Louis Renou

SB- 6 *The Essence of Ancient Philosophy* by André Cresson

SB- 7 *A History of Alchemy* by Serge Hutin

SB- 8 *Surrealism* by Yves Duplessis

SB- 9 *The Churches of the West* by Marcel Pacaut

SB-10 *A History of Judaism* by André Chouraqui

SB-11 *A History of Magic* by Jérôme-Antoine Rony

SB-12 *Socrates* by Jean Brun

SB-13 *Hitler's Germany* by Claude David

SB-14 *Sexual Reproduction* by Louis Gallien

SB-15 *Memory and Forgetting* by Jean-Claude Filloux

SB-16 *Aerodynamics* by Jacques Lachnitt

SB-17 *Psychoanalysis* by Daniel Lagache

SB-18 *Longevity* by Jacques Guillerme

SB-19 *The Psychology of Animals* by Jean-Claude Filloux

SB-20 *Probability and Certainty* by Emile Borel

SB-21 *Nuclear Radiations* by Marc Lefort

SB-22 *The Earth and the Moon* by Jean Taillé

SB-23 *The Origins of Life* by Jules Carles

SB-24 *Animal Migration* by René Thévenin

SB-25 *Russian Literature* by Marcelle Ehrhard

SB-26 *Chinese Literature* by Odile Kaltenmark

SB-27 *Indian Literature* by Louis Renou

SB-28 *A History of Asia* by René Grousset

SB-29 *A History of Byzantium* by Paul Lemerle

SB-30 *Life in the Middle Ages* by Geneviève d'Haucourt

WALKER SUN BOOKS
continued

SB-31 *Matter, Electricity and Energy* by Geneviève Darmois

SB-32 *Cosmic Rays* by André Cachon, Alice Daudin and Louis Jauneau

SB-33 *Hypnosis and Suggestion* by Paul Chauchard

SB-34 *Microbes* by André Boivin

SB-35 *Genetics and Heredity* by Maurice Caullery

SB-36 *Biological Rhythms* by Alain Reinberg and Jean Ghata

SB-37 *A History of Biology* by Maurice Caullery

SB-38 *Race and Human Migrations* by Louis Dollot

SB-39 *Language and Thought* by Paul Chauchard

SB-40 *The Origin of Species* by Emile Guyénot

A History of Byzantium

/ A SUN BOOK

A History of Byzantium

PAUL LEMERLE

Member of the French School of Athens;
Professor at the Sorbonne

Translated by Antony Matthew / A SUN BOOK

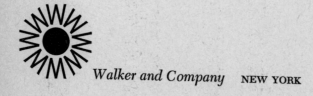

Walker and Company   NEW YORK

First published in France as *Histoire de Byzance*, a volume in the *Que sais-je?* series. © 1960, Presses Universitaires de France.

Copyright © this translation 1964 by Walker and Company, a division of Publications Development Corporation.

Published simultaneously in Canada by George J. McLeod, Limited, Toronto.

Library of Congress Catalog Card Number: 63-13757

MANUFACTURED IN THE UNITED STATES OF AMERICA

To the memory of Stéphane Binon, Belgian member of the French School of Athens, killed at Wakken, May 26, 1940.

PREFACE

This book sketches in broad outline the history of the empire
of which Byzantium was the capital. It seems natural, then,
to begin on May 11, 330, the day on which Constantine solemnly inaugurated the new capital of his empire on the banks
of the Bosphorus, and to conclude on May 29, 1453, the day
that saw the last Byzantine emperor killed fighting on the
battlements, and the entry of the Turks into the city.

I am aware of the criticism I shall invite by beginning in
330. Of course the "Roman" Empire did not come to a sudden
end on that date, to be followed immediately or replaced by
a "Byzantine" one. It could be argued that the year 395, that
of the death of Theodosius and the partition of the empire
between Arcadius and Honorius, might be better. Some authorities would date the empire's beginnings with the reign
of Justinian (527-565), or even that of Leo III (717-740).
These are fruitless arguments. The empire can be called By-

zantine from the moment the emperor, (he remained "Emperor of the Romans" until 1453) abandoned Rome, whose decadence seemed irremediable, and transferred his capital to Constantinople, which became the administrative and political center. During the slow and long evolution by which the empire of Augustus was transformed into an Oriental and Christian monarchy, there are perhaps some dates more important, but there are none more distinctive.

It is equally useless to wrangle about what sort of name we should give to the empire. The French scholars of the seventeenth century who founded Byzantine studies speak simply of "Byzantine history"; it was the eighteenth-century French philosophers of the Enlightenment who threw everything into confusion by mingling history and polemic. They saw fit to condemn Byzantium as the archetype of an absolute monarchy and church state. Voltaire set the tone when he wrote: "Only one period of history is more absurd than Roman history after Tacitus, and that period is Byzantine. This unworthy collection contains nothing but orations and miracles. It is a disgrace to human reason, as Greek imperialism was a disgrace to civilization. The Turks at least were more sensible: they won battles, enjoyed life and wrote very little."

From this judgment, pronounced out of ignorance and bias, Byzantine history has not yet fully recovered. The prejudice was formed that Byzantium was merely a pale survivor of the Roman Empire, continuing the wasting process to inevitable collapse in the midst of squabbling monks and the esoteric rituals of an almost barbaric court. Condemned without a hearing, the error of Byzantium was that she had no great historian like Thucydides or Tacitus; for her, there were only chroniclers whose Greek is often difficult. It is simpler to despise them than to read them.

I hope to show here that this empire, ringed through eleven centuries by growing powers in the East and the West, yet resisting the attacks of both and fulfilling alongside them her historical and civilizing mission, deserves better than indifference and contempt.

P. L.

CONTENTS

Preface　　　　　　　　　　　　　　　　　　　　　　　　ix

1. **Constantine; The Christian and Oriental Monarchy**　　　3

   *The Crisis of the Third Century • Diocletian and the
   First Reforms • Constantine's Re-Creation of Imperial
   Unity • Constantine and Christianity • The Founding
   of Constantinople • The Constantinian Monarchy and
   the Empire of the Fourth Century*

2. **From Constantine to Justinian: The Struggle against the**　29
   Heretics and Barbarians
   *General Points • Religious Problems • The End of
   Paganism • Christianity as a State Religion •
   Nestorius and the Council of Ephesus • Monophysitism
   and the Council of Chalcedon • The Problem of the
   Barbarians*

3. **The Century of Justinian (518-610)**　　　　　　　　45
   *General Characteristics • Foreign Policy • Internal
   Achievements*

4. **The Dynasty of Heraclius and the End of the Roman**　65
   Empire (610-717)
   *General Characteristics • The Decline of Persia •
   The Settlement of the Slavs in Greece • The Beginnings
   of Bulgaria • The Arab Conquests • The Themes
   and the Militarization of the Empire • The General
   Transformation of the Empire*

5. **The Isaurian and Amorian Dynasties;**　　　　　　77
   Iconoclasm (717-867)
   *The Emperors • The Arabs • The Bulgars and the
   Russians • Iconoclasm*

6. **The Macedonian Dynasty and the Imperial Zenith**　87
   (867-1081)
   *The Emperors • The Arabs in East and West • The
   Bulgarians and the Danube Frontier • The Social
   Problem • The Schism • The Civilization • The
   Decline*

7. **Byzantium and the Crusades; The Dynasties of the Comneni and the Angeli; The Latin States and the Greek Empire of Nicaea (1081-1261)**   103
The Dynasty of the Comneni • The Orient and the Balkans • The West: Venetians and Normans • The First Crusades • The Fourth Crusade • The Latin States • The Empire of Nicaea

8. **The Palaeologi and the Fall of the Byzantine Empire (1261-1453)**   119
General Characteristics • Michael VIII Palaeologus • The Early Successors of Michael VIII • The Last Palaeologi

Conclusion   133

Bibliography   137

Index   139

MAPS

I. **The Empire of Justinian**   56-57

II. **The Empire after the Conquests of the Macedonian Emperors**   92-93

III. **The Greek Orient after the Crusades**   110-111

A History of Byzantium

/ A SUN BOOK

1 / CONSTANTINE; THE CHRISTIAN AND ORIENTAL MONARCHY

The reign of Constantine saw the pagan empire beco. ɘ Christian and Rome's supremacy successfully challenged by Constantinople; it marks clearly the beginning of Byzantine history. But we should stress that there is no clear division between Roman and Byzantine history: for nearly three centuries, until the failure of Justinian to re-create imperial unity, the one appears as the continuation of the other. It was during these three centuries that the Roman and Greek heritage, threatened by the invading barbarians, was gradually transferred to Byzantium. At that time the empire received its most profound influences and its essential Byzantine characteristics.

The Crisis of the Third Century

Like all great events, this had its origin in the past; it is not paradoxical to maintain that the seeds of Constantine's monarchy lay in the empire of Augustus. But let us consider the third century alone. After the brilliance of the Antonine dynasty and that wonderful second century of *Pax Romana*, the empire underwent a disastrous period, which almost caused its downfall. There was an internal crisis: emperors were made and unmade at the whim of soldiers or by bribery; some held power only a few days, and almost all died a violent death. The great weakness of the regime set up by Augustus was never better demonstrated: there was no rule for deciding the succession.

Another crisis was provoked from outside: all along the immense frontiers barbarians attacked and burst through the boundary walls built by Hadrian; Italy itself was threatened. It was in order to make Rome at least less vulnerable to attack that Aurelian built his powerful ramparts.

There was an economic crisis, too. Commerce came to a halt; land was abandoned or devastated; taxation no longer brought in revenue; and the currency was devaluated.

Finally, there was a religious and moral crisis. Old-fashioned paganism, such as Augustus had tried to revive, had for some time been unable to satisfy restless minds. Sects and superstitions of the East spread throughout the empire; the most exotic beliefs and bizarre rites were found side by side and confused with one another. People's inclinations turned toward a religion detached from this world of illusion; they sought the meaning and purpose of existence on earth in the world beyond. Monotheism attracted the best minds, and Christianity quietly succeeded in providing itself with an organization and a creed.

The third century saw several energetic emperors, or rather, emperors full of good intentions: almost all were butchered by their soldiers before they could achieve anything worthwhile. Besides, they were all forced to devote what little time the legions graciously allowed them to scurrying from frontier to frontier, blocking up the largest breaches through which the waters of barbarian invasion were incessantly pouring. It was not until the reign of Diocletian (285-305) that there appeared a man of will strong enough to arrest imperial declines: by introducing bold reforms he showed that he had learned lessons from nearly a century of turmoil.

Diocletian and the First Reforms

It is not only as the predecessor of Constantine that Diocletian deserves our attention: it was he who actually saved the empire, by introducing reforms in many ways as far-reaching as those of Augustus or Hadrian. Indeed Constantine only continued, completed and launched work begun by Diocletian, and at times it is difficult to decide which emperor had the original idea.

Diocletian made of the emperor a sacred figure, worshiped according to precisely ordered rituals borrowed from the ceremonies of Oriental courts; visitors prostrated themselves before him and kissed the hem of his crimson robe. Diocletian carried to extremes the principle of absolute monarchy, and the administrative centralization that went with it. The Senate no longer had an effective role, and its decrees were suppressed.

The provinces controlled by the Senate disappeared with the last special privileges of Italy. The whole government of the empire was now put into the hands of an imperial executive, an imperial civil service and a system of personal imperial agents.

Remembering from earlier times the dangers to which anarchy had exposed the empire, Diocletian rigorously separated civil and military offices, depriving provincial governors of their troops, and generals of all part in administration.

Diocletian finally found it imperative to resolve the two problems on which the safety of the empire depended: the defense of the realm and the regulation of the succession. It was undoubtedly to resolve the first (because he understood it was impossible for one emperor alone to defend the immense frontier) that in 286 he bestowed on Maximian the title "Augustus."[1] Diocletian entrusted Maximian with the defense of the West while he himself kept guard in the East. (We should note in passing the division toward which the empire was inevitably moving: already the predominance of the Greek Orient over the Latin Occident was recognized.)

In 293, to create that system of succession previously lacking, Diocletian transformed this dual division of power into a fourfold one: he gave to each "Augustus" a "Caesar" as an assistant (Constantius Chlorus and Galerius Maximianus). At the outset they were to assist the two emperors in their administration, but they were also intended to be their future successors.

Diocletian wanted to see the system he had created come into operation. So, when he divided the empire with Maximian, he laid down one condition: that Maximian should abdicate when he himself gave up power. This event, not the least remarkable of a splendid reign, took place in 305. Diocletian retired into the magnificent palace Oriental he had built for himself at Spalato, and Constantius Chlorus

---

[1] The title taken by Octavius Caesar when he obtained supreme power. It was later adopted by all Roman emperors. The title means "majestic" or "venerable."

and Galerius Maximianus became emperors, with the hallowed title "Augustus."

Constantine's Re-Creation of Imperial Unity

When Constantius Chlorus became "Augustus" in the West as a result of the abdication of Maximian, a comparatively unknown officer, Severus, was assigned to him as "Caesar." This choice upset the ambitions of two young men: Maxentius, the son of Maximian, and Constantine, the son of Constantius Chlorus by his first marriage (he had married a commoner, said to be a serving girl in an inn, called Helena). The death of Constantius Chlorus in 306 was the signal for a series of crises and attempts to seize power. Constantine had himself proclaimed "Augustus" by the legions of Gaul and Britain; Maxentius had himself proclaimed "*Princeps*" (ruler) at Rome, and later "Augustus" by the Praetorian Guard. After some years of extreme confusion Constantine and Maxentius came face to face in 311.

In the East, the abdication of Diocletian had resulted in Galerius becoming "Augustus"; he took for his assistant an officer called Maximinus Daia, who was given the title of "Caesar." All went according to plan until the death of Galerius in May, 311. At that point Maximinus discovered a competitor in Licinius, to whom Galerius had given the title of "Augustus" in the West during the period of crisis. Yet Licinius had never been able to set foot in the West; his hope was that he would be able to compensate himself in the East for the loss of the office.

From then on events unfolded in logical fashion. In the West, Constantine got rid of Maxentius; in the East Licinius did the same with Maximinus Daia. The battle that gave the West to Constantine took place on October 28, 312, at the

Red Rocks, where the Milvian bridge crosses the Tiber not far from Rome. Maxentius was drowned, and Constantine made a triumphal entry into Rome. In the East, Maximinus Daia was defeated by Licinius near Adrianople at the beginning of 313; he fled to Asia Minor, dying there from illness or poisoning.

Licinius and Constantine apparently reached agreement. In 317 they decided to name as their "Caesars" for one half of the empire two sons of Constantine, Crispus and Constantine the Younger, and for the other, a son of Licinius, Licinius the Younger. It was a momentous step, for with it began the substitution of the hereditary principle for that of delegation, at a time when general opinion seemed to want a restoration of Diocletian's regime. It naturally resulted in each of the "Augusti" seeking supreme power for his family. Much more than the religious issues that we will discuss later, it helped to precipitate the war that broke out in 324. Licinius was defeated at Adrianople and again at Chrysopolis and was forced to surrender to Constantine, who, in spite of his assurances, had him put to death. The same fate awaited Licinius the Younger some time later.

Constantine was now sole emperor. He had already made his third son, Constantius, "Caesar," thus establishing the hereditary principle in imperial succession at the same time he re-established unity. Nothing remained of the system of fourfold division of power.

Constantine and Christianity

Outline of the Problem. Before Constantine, the Roman Empire was pagan; after him, it was Christian. This change was one of the most important in Roman history, but it was also one of Rome's most intricate problems. The fact in itself is undeniable: Christian tradition was not wrong when it put Constantine and his mother Helena among its saints. But early Christian tradition made a tale already full of astonishing happenings more incredible than ever.

The history of Constantine's reign raises the problem of sources, and to this no satisfactory solution was reached until recently. Originally, the document considered most important, at least as to Constantine's relations with Christianity, was a *Life of Constantine* published under the name of the Christian writer Eusebius of Caesarea. But recent studies—in particular those of the great Belgian Byzantine scholar H. Gregoire—have established that, though this biography as it has come to us perhaps contains a core of Eusebius' work, vast parts of it are certainly of a later period. As regards accuracy, we ought to treat with the greatest suspicion a text that may well be, not the work of a contemporary with personal knowledge of Constantine, but a compilation from the end of the fourth or the beginning of the fifth century.

Let us take one example, that of the famous vision which preceded the battle against Maxentius at the Milvian bridge. The traditional story is well known: a glowing cross appeared in the sky, with the words "By this sign thou shalt conquer"; Constantine ordered the soldiers to draw this sign on their shields; conversion to Christianity and the victory followed. This is all found in the *Life*, but not in any other text contemporary with Constantine. More serious is the fact that this incident is ignored by the Fathers of the Church up to and including Saint Augustine. What likelihood is there of the story being true, unless we admit that everything concerning the vision is apocryphal?

The only texts that can be safely relied on, if we include the official panegyrics, are the *Ecclesiastical History* of Eusebius (which is not suspect, and besides makes no mention of the vision), and the tract of Lactantius, *On the Death of the Persecutors*. If we add archaeological evidence, inscriptions and information gathered from coins, it is possible to reconstruct an account that, while far from definitive, is a long way from the traditional story. It runs somewhat as follows.

Sun-Worship and Christianity. Constantine began his life as a pagan, a devotee of sun worship. The first and perhaps the only vision that he saw was pagan. We know this from an address delivered in praise of Constantine in his presence at Trier in 310: in a sanctuary in Gaul, Apollo appeared to Constantine, and with him the goddess of victory, bearing laurel crowns among which was a symbol that Constantine interpreted as a prophecy that his reign would be long. This vision was to play an important role in his life: if he was not already a fervent worshiper of the sun, he became one and remained so for a long time. His coins bear evidence of this, in particular those that show the figures of Constantine and the sun god side by side on the same piece.

Yet the situation for Christians in the empire was to change completely without Constantine having any hand in it. It was Galerius who, in 311, issued the real edict of tolerance that declared Christianity a recognized religion and granted Christians the right of assembly, provided they did not distrub the peace. In exchange for this right they were asked to pray to their God for the prosperity of the emperor and the state. The explanation of this edict, surprising if one remembers that Galerius had once severely persecuted Christians, is perhaps to be found in a mental disturbance that

Galerius suffered when attacked by some terrible disease which was to bring about his death not long afterward. But it also seems likely that people were tired of the persecutions, the futility of which was only too evident. Whatever the reason, this was undoubtedly a true edict of tolerance. It is unfortunate that a tradition persists which gives the credit to what is called—very incorrectly, as we shall see—the Edict of Milan.

The following year, 312, was the year of the famous battle of the Milvian bridge. We already know that we must rule out the account which appears in the pseudo-Eusebian *Life of Constantine*. There are two remaining authorities: Lactantius and the *Ecclesiastical History*. The latter makes no mention of the vision or of anything like it. Lactantius speaks not of an apparition of a glowing cross but of a simple dream. In it Constantine, on the eve of the battle, was enjoined to order his soldiers to inscribe on their shields a letter X crossed by a bar incurved at the top. Certain scholars, Gregoire among them, also reject the tale of Lactantius, seeing in it another version of the pagan vision of 310. Others think they can accept it because they find in it an explanation of Constantine's emblem, which was later interpreted as the first two Greek letters of the name of Christ. But in all this nothing allows us to declare that Constantine was a Christian in 312.

Christian tradition attaches no less importance to the following year, 313, that of the Edict of Milan; clear proof, it is said, of the conversion of Constantine. But what really happened? At Milan in 313 there were meetings between Constantine, the conqueror of Maxentius, and Licinius, who was preparing to oust Maximinus Daia. Was one of the subjects of these meetings the policy to be followed on the Christian question? We can make this supposition, but we cannot be sure. We do possess, however, two documents from the period. Lactantius has handed down to us the Latin text of a decree issued in June, 313, by Licinius; it was addressed to the governor of Bithynia and stamped at Nicomedia. Eusebius has the Greek text of the same ordinance in his *Ecclesiastical History*. Without in the least putting the Christian religion before all others, the decree affirms liberty of conscience, and with a desire to pacify as well as act justly, orders that confiscated property be restored to the Christians. This is in fact the document known as the "Edict of Milan" on which Constantine has been so much congratulated. More precisely, it should be called the "Ordinance of Nicomedia"; it is actually an ordinance made by Licinius and intended to be enforced in the East.

The second document is a prayer, also preserved by Lactantius. It was composed by Licinius (or, according to Lactantius, revealed to Licinius), who taught it to his soldiers and had them recite it before the decisive battle against Maximinus Daia. It is in no way a Christian text in the true sense, although nothing in it would have offended a Christian; it is an invocation to a Supreme Being whom the devotees of Mithra and the sun as well as the Christians could consider to be their god.

These are the two texts that give some indication of the way the emperors were thinking in 313. But we should note that both documents can be attributed to Licinius and both concern the East; it seems likely that, occupied as he was with the struggle against Maximinus Daia, Licinius was hoping in this way to win over to his cause the important Christian communities of the East. As for Constantine, it is very likely that he knew and approved of these texts: he himself, perhaps with similar feelings before an equally decisive battle (against Maxentius a few months before), seems to have countered the innumerable pagan rites performed by his enemy with protestations of tolerance and invocations to a god whom the Christians could recognize as their own. But we cannot be sure; authentic evidence that has come down to us from 313, in the form of a gold medallion struck in the imperial workshop at Tarragon, shows the twin figures of Constantine and the sun god. It seems unlikely that Constantine was already converted in the full sense of the word at this date.

The Conversion of Constantine. Some recent studies, based particularly on the evidence of coins, lead us to think that Constantine did not show any clear leaning toward Christianity until after 320. Whether this was the result of personal conviction, or even perhaps of the approaching conflict with Licinius, is uncertain. The pseudo-Eusebian *Life* considers that Licinius' persecution of the Christians in the East was the motive for the war, but this is blatantly inaccurate. Yet it is possible that the struggle, in which Constantine's ambition undoubtedly played a decisive part, ended by taking on the appearance of, among other things, a religious conflict. Perhaps the defeat of Licinius at Adrianople in 324 seemed a defeat for paganism, as the victory of Constantine seemed a victory for Christianity. But what should be noted is that after his victory Constantine never sought to impose Christianity as the official religion. If we are to believe the pseudo-Eusebius (who is only suspect in that he exaggerates Constantine's leaning to Christianity), the emperor sent a proclamation to the peoples of the East after his victory, declaring every man free to follow his own belief.

Great care, then, must be taken in speaking of the "conversion" of Constantine. It should not be forgotten that Constantine was converted to the Christian faith in slow stages; several circumstances contributed to this, but political considerations were more important than personal revelation. For some time Christianity appeared to him merely as superior to other current religions, but in no way essentially different; indeed, throughout the whole of his reign he remained *pontifex maximus* (high priest), and even if he wanted to rid paganism of its defects and most glaring superstitions, he did not try to denigrate it.

On the other hand, it would be futile to deny that Constantine was always concerned with the question of Christianity; from the beginning he showed great tolerance toward Christians, and this soon changed to favoritism. It is clear also that at some point Constantine was converted, for it is recorded that he was baptized. And though he put off receiving the sacrament of baptism until he was dying, this should not necessarily be taken as a sign of indifference: the custom was quite common at the time, since it was believed that in this way one erased more completely the errors of one's life. What is surprising is that Constantine was baptized by an *Arian* bishop.

Constantine and the Church.   A religion like Christianity, which lives and flourishes by independent vitality, needs nothing more than freedom and safety; and Constantine, in the full knowledge of what he was doing, gave it both. As a consequence the Roman world became covered with churches. In the heart of the growing Christian communities intense theological activity developed. Unfortunately, heresies grew in the same proportion. We shall pass over the less important of these, even Donatism (although it gave Constantine the first opportunity to intervene in the affairs of the church), and shall concentrate on Arianism. This is the name given to a doctrine that probably originated in the third century in Syria, in any case, it was developed in the fourth century by Arius, a priest from Alexandria. Arius would not admit that the three persons of the Trinity were equal, but maintained that if the Father, or God, was really eternal and not begotten, the Son was a creation of the Father. He thus denied the doctrine of consubstantiality and, indirectly, the divinity of Christ. As a result of this he was excommunicated by the Bishop of Alexandria; the decision was confirmed by one synod, only to be annulled by another. The whole of the Christian East was divided over the dispute, and Constantine decided to intervene, doubtless mainly for the sake of peace.

As he was unable to reconcile the protagonists, in 325 he brought together a body of men in what was to be the first ecumenical council. After several months the bishops agreed to a text that all but two of them signed. This was the Nicaean Creed. It clearly stated that the Son is of one substance with the Father (in Greek *homoousios*). The importance of this council was not only that it set out for the first time the dogma of the Trinity and laid the doctrinal foundation for the Christian religion, but also that it marked the first time imperial power had intervened in a question of doctrine; all future relations between the temporal and the spiritual were to follow from this. We make a special point of the *temporal*, for it was only in his capacity as temporal ruler (we might almost speak of his police power) that Constantine intervened. He seems to have had no other aim than to maintain peace and order in the Christian Church, which had become one of the focal points of the empire. His conduct after the council proves this: he took the initiative in executing these decisions himself, personally exiling Arius and his most turbulent collaborators. That he was guided by a concern for what was politic rather than by personal conviction is better shown by his attitude to the Arian question in the following years.

Nothing illustrates Constantine's temperament better. So energetic in action, so unbending in the measures he took to enforce public morality (he punished adultery and political informing severely), he was nevertheless in other ways a procrastinator, easily influenced and inclined to change his mind continually after he had made a decision. This was perhaps because of his scrupulous attention to justice. A few years after the Council of Nicaea, Arianism was revived, and Arius himself recalled from exile. At the same time, his chief opponent, Athanasius of Alexandria, was sent into exile. What were Constantine's guiding principles in this? Perhaps he had discovered that Arianism, in the West at least, was stronger than orthodoxy. Perhaps he had doubts about the decisions reached at Nicaea. Nothing is known definitely, but it is thought that he was under the influence of his sister Constantia, who was closely in league with the Arian archbishop, Eusebius of Nicodemia. In fact it was the latter who baptized Constantine on his deathbed. But at the same time, as a final contradiction, he recalled Athanasius, Arius' enemy, from exile.

These charactertistics complete the outstandingly complex figure of Constantine, insofar as he was a Christian. What is absolutely certain is that he was not a Christian pure and simple, as certain traditions would have us believe. On the subject of religion, if we wanted to draw up the balance

sheet of his reign, we could say that Christians were t persecuted but treated with benevolence; that their gious
practice was no longer forbidden, but made lawful hat in
law Christianity was not favored at the expense of anism
but was clearly put in a position where it could su lant it;
that Christianity was not a state religion but a reli on with
privileges; and that for the first time an emperor received
baptism, and a government concerned itself with th internal
affairs of the Church. This is undoubtedly sufficien to justify
the eminent place that Christian tradition gives C nstantine.

The Founding of Constantinople

We must define our terms exactly when spe ing of the
founding of Constantinople by Constantine. Th situation
was not one of a town being built on a new site: the ancient
Megarian colony of Byzantium already occupied the tip of
this almost triangular island that juts out between the Sea of
Marmara and the vast natural harbor of the Golden Horn.
For a long time Byzantium had owed its prosperity, no less
than the changing fortunes of its history, to this exceptionally
convenient position on the great trade route of the Straits, the
corn route of antiquity, and the meeting place of Europe and
Asia Minor. But it was no more than a large provincial town
when Constantine chose it as a second capital for the empire.

Before Constantine the Roman world had one capital,
Rome; after him it had, in theory, two, Rome and Constantinople. But in reality, while Rome was abandoned to its decline, Constantinople grew continually in stature; the fact
that it was the residence of the emperor and the seat of the
administration made it the real capital. This move was the
crucial event of Constantine's reign, much more important

even than his conversion to Christianity, which only speeded up the inevitable.

Ever since ancient times it has been said that Constantine left the pagan citadel of Rome because he felt he had no popularity there. This is untrue, just as it is untrue to say (as does the testimony of the pseudo-Eusebius) that Constantine wanted to make Constantinople a Christian city. The "founding" of the city was accompanied by pagan rituals; if Constantine had churches built there, he let the temples remain; and indeed (according to the reports of the pagan Zosimus, generally reliable) he may even have constructed new ones. In fact, he acted in accordance with strategic, economic and political considerations.

Strategic. The most serious threats facing the empire came from the Goths and the Persians. Rome, besides being itself vulnerable to the Germanic and Illyrian tribes, was much too far away from these two centers of military activity. Constantinople, itself extremely difficult to capture, was at the same time an excellent operational base for land and sea action against the barbarians of the North and the East.

Economic. It was necessary in difficult times to maintain free passage through the Straits, and to safeguard trade between the Mediterranean and the river states on the Black Sea, between Europe and Asia Minor.

Political. The general decadence of Italy, already so apparent in the second century, had only worsened. Rome, proudly frozen in its ancient privileges, was a dead city, and the Greek Orient, by its wealth and civilization, clearly appeared to be the vital half of the empire.

Indeed, since the third century Rome had ceased to be the real seat of government. It is significant that of the four rulers of the four divisions of the empire, not one had his residence there; even in Italy at that period, Milan had already superseded Rome. Constantine never lived there; instead he resided at Trier, at Sirmium (Mitrovica), at Sardica (Sofia) and at Nicomedia—all stages on the great route from West to East, a route that went through Constantinople but bypassed Italy.

In 324, when victory over Licinius delivered the Eastern Empire to him, Constantine, with a stroke of genius, chose Byzantium. The construction work began at once and lasted until 336, giving employment to a considerable number of workers (at one point 40,000 Goths were employed on the job). Many great towns were stripped of their art treasures, and many historic buildings of their columns or statues, in order to decorate the new city. To attract eminent Romans, gifts were made of completely new town palaces; and for the general public the emperor set up the *annona* (a kind of dole), as in Rome, and made free distributions of corn. He himself outlined the boundaries of the city, giving it a total area four or five times that of ancient Byzantium. The solemn inauguration ceremony took place before the work was finished, on May 11, 330. From that time on the emperor lived at Constantinople, and the imperial government had its seat there. The city, which was named after Constantine, was often also called New Rome. The name persisted. Like Rome, Constantinople was built on seven hills, and had fourteen regions; there was a forum, a capitol and a senate; moreover, its territory was legally Italian soil, not a province, and therefore exempt from taxation. Rome did not yet lose any of its privileges, but all were now shared and Constantinople was the gainer. Very naturally it soon became the true capital;

Rome was gradually neglected, alone and forgotten, vainly repeating the empty gestures of its glorious past. As Louis Bréhier puts it: "On the coins of 330 the two towns appear in the form of the busts of figures wearing laurel wreaths and helmets covered with an imperial cloak; but it is Constantinople that holds the scepter."

The consequences were enormous: immediate rivalry began between the Latin West, which seemed to have been abandond to its state of incurable decay, and the Greek East. The foundation of Constantinople marks the victory of the East over the West, of a certain kind of Hellenism, very orientalized, over the Latin spirit.

It was also the starting point of a new civilization, which can properly be called "Byzantine." No other city in history (except perhaps Rome) has had such a powerful and lasting effect as Constantinople. Although the empire was to be threatened, attacked and invaded on all sides, yet for eleven centuries Constantinople withstood all. Under the protection of her walls, in palaces, monasteries and workshops, there mingled the Greco-Latin, Christian and Oriental elements from which was shaped the Byzantine civilization.

One has only to imagine what might have happened if Constantinople had not been founded when Rome, whose collapse was unavoidable and imminent, sank under the flood of the barbarian invasion. The entire heritage of ancient civilization might have disappeared with her; indeed, for several centuries it did disappear in the West. No other city was capable of centralizing the classical tradition, not even Antioch or Alexandria. Besides, the Arab conquests were on the way. As soon as Constantinople was founded it attracted all that remained vital in the Greco-Latin civilization. Throughout its entire history, thanks to its power, wealth, prestige and the very fact that it preserved the Greek language, Constantinople preserved its inheritance. By this timely shift of the center of the empire, Constantine saved all that could be saved. It is for this that he deserves the greatest credit.

The Constantinian Monarchy and the Empire of the Fourth Century

It is well to remember that toward the middle of the three-century period that separated Augustus and Constantine, the Roman Empire had undergone the far-reaching reforms of Hadrian. Recruitment to the army had been regionalized; the ruler's advisory council and the imperial secretariat had been reorganized; the administration of Italy had been taken away from the Senate; and a hierarchy of office, salary and title had been set up for the equestrian order.[2] All these were significant measures for the future. Diocletian also instituted reforms, which on many points have been confused with Constantine's. Once these reservations have been made, it can be said with truth that Constantine deserves the credit for giving definite form to what had previously been merely sketched out. By the end of his reign the empire had in all details received entirely new characteristics. From that moment a new history begins.

The Empire and its Defense. Geographically the boundaries of the empire had undergone little change. In Europe, Roman authority extended over all the territory to the west and south of the Rhine and the Danube, and over Britain with the exception of what are today Scotland and

[2] The rich merchant class, consisting of families whose members, though rich, had not achieved high government office.

Ireland; in Africa, it included a coastal band of varying width extending from Morocco (Mauritania) up to and including Egypt; in Asia, the Sinai Peninsula, Palestine, Syria and Asia Minor. Its boundaries in the east were the Arabian Desert, the Persian Empire and the upper valleys of the Euphrates and Tigris rivers. Within these frontiers the territory was divided into over 100 provinces, between which all administrative differences had been wiped out. Diocletian had grouped the provinces into twelve dioceses, which were themselves soon grouped into prefectures: Gaul, Italy, Illyria and the Orient.

The defense of the empire was organized according to a new system. There had been a theory that, to protect imperial territory, one should build a sort of Chinese wall of continuous fortifications all along the frontiers, behind which shelter the empire would find security. But little by little towns had spread out into the neighboring plains and left the walls to crumble into ruins. The invasions of the third century showed the weakness of this system. Under powerful barbarian pressure the boundary system collapsed, leaving the open towns defenseless within; for this reason towns began to repair their walls or hastily construct them. Again for the same reason, from the time of Constantine on, the main defense of the empire was not concentrated on the frontier, where only a token force of peasant soldiers, the *Limitanei,* was retained, but in strongholds with permanent garrisons. The policy was very sound, since the barbarians were more numerous and highly mobile, always able to penetrate at some point the feeble barrier on the borders. But they understood nothing of siege warfare and did not know how to capture a fort.

The Emperor and the Government. The emperor was

an absolute sovereign; he was God. In the third century Aurelian had already worn the crown in public, the prerogative of the gods. Inscriptions give him the title of *deus et dominus*. The inevitable evolution of the state toward a monarchy on the Oriental model, under the influence of Hellenistic, Egyptian and Persian monarchies, was completed with Diocletian and Constantine. There was scrupulous attention to the rituals of adoration for the ruler, and at the same time everything that concerned the emperor became sacred: the minister of finance, from the moment when the emperor's fortune was identified with that of the empire, became the "Comptroller of the Sacred Bounty"; the chief of the imperial wardrobe became the "Master of the Sacred Robes."

This new conception of the emperor implied a new conception of imperial administration and government. It depended on two notions: first, the imperial palace, the "court," as we say, became the center of the state and the empire; secondly, men no longer served the state but the emperor. The Oriental and later the medieval idea of personal service to the prince took the place of the ancient idea of service to an office. Here also we must take care not to speak of a revolution: Roman emperors had always had "clients" or "friends." From them Hadrian had already recruited his advisory council, which had gradually taken the place of the Senate. But from the time of Constantine the institution received its definite form: important state offices were conferred on the emperor's "companions" (Latin, *comites*; French, *comtes*).

To avoid confusion among this ever-increasing horde of people circulating around the emperor, it was necessary to establish meticulous rules of *precedence*. The system was exactly the reverse of what had existed in Rome. There, for a long time, the function one fulfilled had depended on the class to which one belonged; but now the class came to depend on the function. Of those who surrounded the emperor, the members of his family were *nobilissimi*. There then followed in order, the *patrices*, the *illustres*, the *spectabiles*; the *clarissimi*—corresponding approximately to the ancient senatorial order—and the *perfectissimi,* the equestrian order. "The Augustan system of fixed rank was replaced by a hierarchy of officials" (E. Albertini).

To avoid the danger of an official becoming too important, and to obviate the dangers of a seizure of power or a rebellion—the previous century had shown the seriousness of these—the separation of military and civil authority, which had been for some time the convention, became the rule. Generals no longer took part in administration; conversely, provincial governors, district administrators and court judges became themselves purely civil servants. Central administration was entrusted to imperial departments under the authority of a Chief Secretary. The organization and the division into four branches, which was Hadrian's legacy, were both preserved in their entirety.

Economic Crisis and Social Change. These far-reaching governmental reforms were accompanied by social changes that affected all classes and walks of life. Their origin must be sought in the economic crisis provoked or aggravated by the disturbances and difficulties of the third century. The slowing down of trade, widespread poverty, the decrease in the number of slaves, and industrial decline all brought about a serious reversal in the economic conditions of life in the empire, until then essentially urban.

For the first three centuries the Roman Empire appeared

as a federation of cities set up with Rome as the model. Each
town received its image from Rome: it was administered by
magistrates and senators who copied the Roman municipal
hierarchy. But this happy balance only lasted while times
were good. Even during the third century imperial officials—
the provincial governor, and especially the financial officer—
had seriously encroached on the authority of the municipali-
ties. The latter saw their responsibilities increased as their
importance diminished. It was traditional for a magistrate to
spend a great deal of money on improving his town and providing for the pleasure of his fellow citizens. As the old families became impoverished, office was less sought after and
high positions became less important and more onerous.
After Diocletion's reforms, when army officers had the task
of assessing and levying taxes, these offices were avoided a
great deal. When Constantine made magistrates personally
responsible for the collection of taxes, with their own money
as a guarantee, citizens refused to take on the responsibility.
The state then intervened to fix the categories of citizens liable for payments to the curia (the local treasury); they were
obliged to accept responsibility for this. In this way a hereditary class of *curiales* was formed. "It was impossible for a son,
on receiving his father's inheritance, not to take on his financial responsibilities as well. . . . The obligation was a hereditary one . . . and he who held it became a slave of the curia,
as the peasant was a slave to the soil" (Ferdinand Lot).

To stay in the towns, once so attractive, was now without
charm. The rich avoided taxation by paying a subscription to
the Senate in the capital, which absolved them from their
obligations to the local curia; this is why admission to the
ranks of the *clarissimi* was so sought after a favor. A new so-

cial class was formed, the great provincial landowners. Living independently on their properties, they managed to escape the authority of the local officials, avoided income tax, often assumed legal powers themselves and took over the right of asylum. Moreover, by the institution of patronage, these landowners attracted some of the best people from the towns, flouting the growing demands of the treasury by taking these people under their protection. The latter in turn generally gave up some of their property, keeping only what they needed for personal use. This was a serious threat to imperial revenue; laws against patronage in response to this were made continually, but they had little success.

The economic crisis reversed the relative importance of town and country: land became the principal source of wealth. It seemed important to prevent its continual exploitation at the whim of individuals, and to organize it for state benefit. The peasants, even more than the *curiales* and the tradesmen of the towns, were chained to their condition and the soil. Of course a peasant, whether working land or owning it, was a free man; but at the same time he was traditionally attached to a piece of land that he had no right to leave, and from which he could not be expelled. This is what was meant by being bonded to the soil.

From the fourth century, soldiers, officials, merchants, urban craftsmen and peasants all had a fixed and often hereditary status. Only the power of the rich or the favor of the emperor brought the possibility of diversity. The most striking characteristic of these social conditions was clearly the authoritarian intervention of the state in all aspects of society. This had become inevitable for two reasons. First, the economic crisis had resulted in a universal attempt to shed responsibilities. In response to this, the state rigorously froze everyone in his position, the better to hold him to his obligations. This was only an expedient, erroneously taken for a cure. But in this gigantic empire with its tremendous variability, where even Rome had been unable to develop a sense of common purpose, there was no salvation but in authoritarian rule. Secondly, it is a fact that the regime created by Augustus failed because he had not given the empire a constitution suited to its size. Augustus could not picture anything but the municipal government of Rome multiplied indefinitely in all cities under Roman sway. What of *Senatus populusque romanus* (the Senate and the Roman people)? Alas, the Senate had been reduced to the rank of a municipal council. As for the people, they had long been a mere caricature of a sovereign public; for them, political struggles had become like gladiatorial shows. So once more there was no other remedy than direction from above.

2 / FROM CONSTANTINE TO JUSTINIAN: THE STRUGGLE AGAINST THE HERETICS AND BARBARIANS

General Points

Constantine had founded a Christian and Oriental empire. For almost two centuries, until the beginning of Justinian's dynasty, the principal task of his successors was to be the defense of Christianity against heretics, and the defense of the East against invaders.

It was a confused epoch: in East and West more than twenty emperors governed in succession, among them Spaniards, Illyrians, Thracians and one Asiatic. Several reigns were either much longer than the others, or more remarkable. After Constantine II, son of Constantine, came his cousin Julian (361-363); at his death the dynasty of Constantius Chlorus came to an end. There followed Valentinian in the West, and Valens in the East. Valens (364-378) was succeeded by a Spaniard, Theodosius (379-395), who received the appellation "the Great." His sons ruled one in the West (Hanorius) the other in the East (Arcadius, 395-408). orcadius was followed by his son Theodosius II (408-450). However, while the West lay open to the barbarian invaders, the East was governed in succession from 450-518 by Marcianus, Leo I, Zeno and Anastasius. In fact, two reigns are particularly important: that of Theodosius I, because he was the last emperor to have effective sway over the whole empire; and that of Theodosius II. Though a somewhat insignificant character, he reigned long enough to allow his ministers and his sister Pulcheria, who governed for him, to carry out much useful work.

During this unsettled period the empire was sometimes in the hands of a single emperor, sometimes divided between two, one in the East and one in the West. Nevertheless the united concept of imperial government remained. It remained so in law because one emperor normally invested the other with office; it remained so in fact because one of the emperors generally had sufficient authority to impose his views on the other. The idea subsisted also in the people's minds. Neither Romans nor barbarians thought of the East and the West as separate: Odoacer called on Anastasius to invest him, which he did. It is not entirely true to say that the death of Theodosius I in 395 produced a partition of the empire between Honorius and Arcadius, and a definite division between the East and the West. Theodosius I was overtaken by death just as, like so many of his predecessors, he had named his heirs: Honorius in the West and Arcadius in the East, but he did not envisage partition, nor did his contemporaries. About forty years later the famous legal code of Theodosius II was published: it combined the constitutions of all the Christian emperors since Constantine. It was also made in the name of the emperor then reigning in the West, Valentinian III, since a constitution of one emperor, to be valid, had to be communicated to his colleague. The concept of the empire as a single unit governed by joint imperial agreement still existed. But even if the constitutional unity of the empire was maintained, it was nonetheless true that rivalry between East and West had increased; indeed, it was the dominant characteristic of the period we are concerned with, for several reasons:

1. *The vitality of the empire lay entirely in the East.* Constantine confirmed this when he founded Constantinople; the extraordinary progress made by the city showed he had been right in doing so. The city grew so rapidly that it was soon too large for its walls, and during the reign of Theodosius II it became necessary to build a new wall of greater length and toughness, fortified on the land side by three lines of defense. This wall was impregnable, and by protecting Constantinople from the barbarians right up to the invention of siege artillery, it played a vital role in Byzantine history. At the same time Theodosius II gave the city a university, endowed with thirty chairs, divided more or less equally between the languages of Greek and Latin. This was doubly interesting: it proved the determination of Constantinople to be equally an intellectual capital, and it put Greek on equal terms with Latin—an equality that was soon to become superiority.

2. *Christianity developed in different ways in East and West.* In the fourth century the highest ecclesiastical authority in the West, Ambrose, Bishop of Milan, proclaimed the independence of the spiritual from the temporal—this at the very time when, in the East, Theodosius I was making Christianity a state religion. In the fifth century Pope Leo the

Great affirmed the supremacy of the seat of Rome, while the twenty-eighth canon of the Council of Chalcedon was bringing about the subjugation of the East to the authority of the Patriarch of Constantinople.

3. *The barbarian invasions did not have the same impact on East and West.* We shall now see how the East, stronger and more capable of defending itself, withstood the invasions, while the West collapsed. As a result the balance between the two parts of the empire, which had become increasingly strained, was finally upset.

Religious Problems

In the fourth and fifth centuries the history of internal affairs is inseparable from that of Christianity; indeed this remains so throughout Byzantine history. We tend to neglect these theological disputes; there is no exact equivalent for them in the history of Western Europe, though the Wars of Religion may perhaps share their violence and political importance. We should remember that the development of the concept of monarchy, which took shape in the fourth and fifth centuries, acquired much moral and social strength from Christianity. At the same time also Christianity itself was showing commendable ability to expand, with Gregory the Illuminator's evangelization of Armenia, and the efforts of Frumentius in Abyssinia and Ulfila among the Goths. We should also mention Persia, where the Nestorians took refuge after they were expelled from the empire.

The End of Paganism

Constantius had favored Christianity in several laws; concurrently he had passed a series of ordinances limiting the activity of pagans. His successor, Julian, had received instruction in both Greek paganism and Christianity and had been baptized; this allowed the Church to give him the title "the Apostate." But in fact Julian had never been a Christian at heart, and doctrinal controversies had only succeeded in alienating him. At the death of Constantius he was recalled from Gaul, where he had campaigned successfully against the Germanic tribes, and made emperor. Julian then allowed his true feelings to show. He passed an edict ordering the temples reopened and sacrifices made to the gods; he also reorganized pagan worship and the priesthood, borrowing numerous features from Christian practice and organization. But he did not persecute the Christians; indeed he even issued a declaration of tolerance, recalling from exile the enemies of Arianism, who had been banished under Constantius. But at the same time he began removing Christians from important state offices, and forbade them to teach in schools. The paganism of Julian was, moreover, very civilized, far removed from the vulgar superstition the Christians took pleasure in denouncing.

In 363 Julian died while commanding an expedition against the Persians. The measures he had taken against Christians were soon revoked, but the pagans were not disturbed. They were able to continue celebrating their rites, it seems, both in East and West, until the reign of Theodosius I.

The latter was a fanatical Christian and convinced, moreover, of the absolute right of the state to control religion. His enactments against paganism culminated in the famous edict of 392 whereby sacrifices and all the rituals of the pagan religion were forbidden, even access to the temples. Those who contravened this were liable to a charge of treason or sacrilege. Temples were demolished by fanatical Christians, or converted into churches; the statues they sheltered were broken or, sometimes, sent to Constantinople to decorate the city. In 393 the Olympic games were prohibited, as were the Eleusinian mysteries three years later. In the East the ritual destruction of the Serapium of Alexandria appears to mark the final abolition of what Theodosius called in his edict "the pagan superstition." In the West the most significant event occurred in the reign of Gratianus, when the altar and the statue of Victory in the Senate at Rome, which symbolized all the greatness of the Roman past, were removed.

Christianity as a State Religion

As we have already seen, Constantine did not follow a well-defined poIicy in the face of Arianism. Among his successors, Constantius and Valerius were Arians, too. Theodosius I, on the other hand, who had been instructed and baptized by a Nicaean bishop, showed himself resolutely opposed to Arianism. Once in power, he banished from Constantinople the Arian bishop and gave all the churches in the city to the Nicaeans. In 380 he issued a law by which only those who followed the Nicaean doctrine of the Trinity could call themselves "Catholics"; the rest, including the Arians, were "heretics." Further edicts deprived "heretics" of the right to assemble for religious ceremonies, and even of certain civil rights. A council called by Theodosius at Constantinople in 391 supported the Nicaean Creed, which affirmed that the Father and the Son were of one substance, completing this by declaring the consubstantiality of the Holy Spirit with the other two Persons. This same council established the status of the Bishop of Constantinople: as Constantinople was the new Rome, its bishop became the most important one after that of Rome. There was no equality with Rome; but already the Bishop of Constantinople was regarded as superior to his fellow bishops in the East.

These decisions were extremely important; they guaranteed to Theodosius I a pre-eminent place in the history of Christianity, alongside Constantine. Theodosius declared in effect that there could be no toleration in religious matters: there was one state religion, its tenets binding and fixed by the emperor, who was to impose them on his subjects. Orthodoxy and heresy became matters of politics as well as of religion, or rather, the two matters were confused. Thus, as far as relations between Church and State were concerned, we see the foundations of the doctrine sometimes inappropriately called *caesaropapism,* henceforth to be the policy of the Byzantine Empire.

This policy of Theodosius was opposed in principle to the idea upheld by Saint Ambrose, the most famous contemporary representative of the Church in the West. The latter was convinced that the affairs of the Church and questions of doctrine should not depend on the views of the temporal power. In this respect it is true to say that Theodosius' attitude nurtured the seeds of the next conflicts between East and West.

Finally, by placing the Bishop of Constantinople above other bishops of the East, the council of 381 was bound to arouse the reaction, futile but obstinate, of the bishops of Antioch and particularly of Alexandria. Thus it played a role in the disputes of the fifth century, whose theological guise often masked worldly interests and conflicts about precedence.

Nestorius and the Council of Ephesus

Under Arcadius, who succeeded Theodosius I in the East, the resolute attitude of the Bishop of Constantinople, John Chrysostomus, assured the triumph of the Nicaean doctrine. He deserves credit for this, for the Gothic faction was at that time all-powerful in Constantinople, and the Goths were Arians. Under Theodosius II, whose long reign included the first half of the fifth century, Christian theological disputes again occurred. The first and one of the most important was that aroused by the Nestorian heresy.

The Council of Nicaea had laid down that Christ was both God and man. Henceforth the argument turned on the way in which the two were united in the person of Christ. At Antioch, which had been the cradle of Arianism, there grew up a doctrine that declared the two natures to be clearly separate; of these the human was the more important, since Christ was only a man become God. When this doctrine was upheld by Nestorius, Patriarch of Constantinople, who had also been a priest at Antioch, it aroused trouble—all the more serious because the dispute was no longer on the theological plane alone. Against Nestorius and his supporters were ranged the bishops of Alexandria, and the struggle was soon to take on political significance.

The prestige of the patriarchal seat of Alexandria was enormous in the East; the power of its occupants was absolute in Egypt. Both of these had been increased by the victory of Athanasius, one of the most eminent Alexandrians, over Arius. The bishops of Alexandria aspired to exercise a kind of religious dominance in the East; they were disturbed by or jealous of the primacy accorded by the Council of Constantinople to the bishop of that city. This largely accounts for their energy and zeal for orthodoxy in the dispute with Nestorius. When in 428 Celestine, Bishop of Rome, condemned the Nestorian doctrine, Cyril, Bishop of Alexandria, had the Egyptian council draw up twelve propositions summarizing orthodoxy that he asked Nestorius to accept under threat of dismissal. Theodosius II, hesitant but wanting to cut short the dispute, with the impression that it was all a plot hatched by the Alexandrians, called another ecumenical council—the third—at Ephesus in 431. At this council Cyril took part in intrigues; his presence inspired fear everywhere; his interference, through his numerous followers, was often brutal. All this, and the presents he distributed among the emperor's entourage, made of the council a personal triumph. Nestorius was deposed from the seat of Constantinople and a successor put in his place. Cyril, on his return to Egypt, became a kind of Pope of the East.

Monophysitism and the Council of Chalcedon

However, the doctrine supported by Cyril and the Alexandrians was not altogether orthodox, either. By dint of belittling the human aspect of Christ, they were not far from recognizing in him only a single nature, the divine. This was *Monophysitism,* in some ways the opposite of the Nestorian and Arian heresies. When this doctrine was preached by a monk from Constantinople, Eutyches, it received the approval of Dioscorus, the Patriarch of Alexandria, who had succeeded Cyril (and who was no less proud and violent than his predecessor). The doctrine, however, met with the immediate opposition of Pope Leo the Great, who was clearly disturbed not only by the probable heresy, but also by the obvious ambitions of the Egyptian patriarchs.

Theodosius II, embarrassed as usual, called a council at Ephesus in 449; this has been given the name of the "Robber Council of Ephesus." Dioscorus in fact behaved even more contemptuously than had Cyril at the council of 431. By his use of violence he succeeded in forcing the council members to recognize the Monophysite doctrine; and the emperor was feeble enough to ratify a decision obtained by these unorthodox means. In this way the latter precipitated the serious religious crisis that was to disturb the empire when he died in 450. To put an end to this, his successor, Marcianus, convoked the fourth ecumenical council (at Chalcedon in 451), at which papal legates were present. This council unhesitatingly blotted out the decisions reached by the "Robber Council of Ephesus" and deposed Dioscorus. It then drew up a declaration of faith (directly inspired by a text of Leo the Great) that defined Christ as a single person with two natures, in conformity with the Nicaean doctrine, and specifically condemned Monophysitism. The Council of Chalcedon has great religious significance, for it is the true foundation of orthodoxy. It also had important political significance. On the one hand it affirmed the authority of the pope: his representatives sat in the front row and their formula, which defined the dual nature of Christ, was adopted; henceforth no one contested the fact that the Bishop of Rome should have the first place in the Church. But at the same time the twenty-eighth canon of the council, against which Leo the Great vainly protested, declared the diocese of Pontus, Asia Minor and Thrace to be under the jurisdiction of the Bishop of Constantinople alone. The latter became a sort of Primate of the Orient. More serious was the fact that the council appeared a clear defeat for the Alexandrians. But Egypt, Syria and even a part of Asia

Minor maintained their allegiance to Monophysitism. There was disobedience at Alexandria and Antioch when attempts were made to enforce the decisions of the council, and it was at this time that the Church in Egypt seems to have abandoned Greek and adopted the Coptic language. Thus theological disputes concealed national rivalries, and already well-established aspirations toward independence found in this a pretext to set a part of the Orient against Constantinople. We see here the dividing line along which, under the impact of the Persian and Arab invasions two centuries later, a part of the empire was to be detached from the rest.

The emperor Zeno (474-491) perceived the danger and attempted to bring about peace. In 482 he proclaimed an edict of unity that managed to avoid mentioning too clearly the two natures; in this it recalled the Council of Chalcedon. The emperor flattered himself that the two factions would accept the edict, but the very opposite happened. Neither Monophysites nor orthodox Christians completely accepted it; the pope himself rejected it and excommunicated and pronounced an anathema against the Patriarch of Constantinople. The latter, Arcasius, retaliated by striking out the name of the pope from the prayers of his Church. This, the first schism between the churches of the East and the West, was to last until 518.

The Problem of the Barbarians

The barbarians had not always tried to force their way into the empire for plunder. The Germanic peoples had nothing but admiration and respect for the grandeur of Rome. They asked to be allowed into the empire as a favor, to share its advantages and wealth. The empire for its part often free-

ly welcomed them to its fields, its army, and even its administration. Sometimes there was a kind of peaceful invasion.
Under Theodosius I, and above all under Arcadius, the Gothic
faction was all-powerful in Constantinople, and its leader,
Gaïnus, even managed to get the favorite Eutropus executed;
but in the end a popular rebellion led to Gaïnus' murder.
Under Marcianus and Leo I, it was the Alain Aspar who governed the East, until the emperor became aware of the danger
through the general unrest. He used fierce Isaurian mountain-
eers to wipe out Aspar and his followers, putting an end to
Gothic influence at Constantinople forever. It was not so easy
to avert the serious danger present in the deep-seated urge of
certain races to migrate. Germanic hordes or other barbarians
were stirred up whenever ambitious chieftains turned up to
exploit these ideas in their own interest. The East could protect itself, but the West perished. We shall see how the Visigoths of Alaric, the Huns of Attila, and the Ostrogoths of
Theodoric, having thrice brought the Orient almost to ruin,
turned their attack on the West, which served as a sacrifice
for the safety of the other half of the empire.

1. *The Visigoths.* For a long time the empire considered it good policy and a remedy for depopulation to settle in
federated states on its territory Germanic tribes that were
making life difficult on the frontiers. Thus, under Valens, over
200,000 Visigoths were incorporated into lower Moesia at one
time. Almost at once, dissatisfied with the hospitality, the
newcomers fomented a revolt: at the battle of Adrianople in
378 the Romans were overwhelmed and Valens was killed.
Theodosius I, however, succeeded in restraining the Visigoths, by imposing a treaty that kept them in a state of federation with the empire. On Theodoric's death, Alaric, the

leader of the Visigoths, again led his bands on a pillaging expedition into Thrace, Macedonia, Thessaly and even the Peloponnesus. Arcadius thought it wise to negotiate; he settled the Visigoths on new lands in Illyricum, and made Alaric military governor there. Was it his plan to thus direct Alaric's attention toward the West? If so, he was successful. After his first attempt in 402, when he was defeated by Stilicho, Honorius' general, Alaric took the offensive again a few years later. In 410 he captured Rome. The Visigoths went on to establish themselves in Gaul and in Spain, but were never to reappear in the East.

2. *The Huns.* Their place was soon taken by a much more formidable horde of people, the Huns, whose progress had brought them to the frontier of the Danube. Theodosius II had already agreed to give them annual tribute in gold, but Attila, on becoming king, was dissatisfied with this. He compelled Theodosius to double the tribute and give him the title of Military Governor. Still unsatisfied, in 441 Attila crossed the Danube, seized Sirmium and Naïssus, and marched on Constantinople. Theodosius, then at war with the Persians, was compelled in 443 to sign a humiliating treaty, by which he agreed that the annual tribute should be trebled and ransom paid to the Huns for the Roman prisoners they had taken. Nonetheless in 447 Attila again crossed the Danube, ravaged Moesia and pushed on to Thermopylae. Negotiations were again carried on. Marcianus was the first who dared to refuse to pay tribute, perhaps because he realized that Attila's ambitions were directed toward the West. The latter did in fact lead his troops westward, where it is known that they fared badly on the field of Catalaunia. When Attila returned in 452 he did not have sufficient strength to make

immediate war against the emperor at Constantinople. In the following year he died, and his kingdom did not long survive him. For the second time the East was saved.

3. *The Ostrogoths.* Byzantine diplomacy was also flexible enough to ward off another threat, from the Ostrogoths. They had been granted land under Leo I, but their leader, Theodoric, proud of some services he had performed for Zeno, showed himself to be more demanding. Dissatisfied with the consular rank that had been conferred on him, Theodoric laid waste the Balkan peninsula and threatened Constantinople. Events moved very quickly in the western part of the empire as well: in 476 Odoacer, a chieftain from the Germanic tribes, defeated Romulus Augustus (the last Augustus of the West of Roman blood) and occupied Italy. He then obtained Zeno's agreement that the government of Italy should be officially delegated to him. Nonetheless, since he was behaving with dangerous independence, Zeno thought of a clever way of punishing him and at the same time ridding himself of Theodoric. Persuading the latter to do battle with Odoacer, he promised him the succession if he won. Theodoric departed with his troops, defeated Odoacer, and took Ravenna. For the third time the Orient was saved.

Theodoric was proclaimed sovereign of Italy and took Ravenna for his capital. He asked the emperor, Anastasius, to recognize and, as it were, legitimize him. At the same time Anastasius conferred on the King of the Franks, Clovis, the rank of consul. Honor was saved: the empire kept its unity, and the emperor his authority. But this was no more than appearance. The East, undivided, found itself more and more clearly opposed by the West, in which Ostrogoths occupied Italy, Franks a great part of Gaul, Visigoths the rest of Gaul and Spain, and Vandals North Africa. In the sixth century, all Justinian's efforts to turn back the course of history and re-establish unity were unsuccessful; after his reign separation was to be final.

3 / THE CENTURY OF JUSTINIAN (518-610)

General Characteristics

In the history of Byzantium the reign of Justinian appears as a monumental error. The error was to interrupt the normal and inevitable course of history. The empire had already become an empire of the Orient. The emperors of the fifth century, while maintaining their theoretical rights in the West, had in fact abandoned the West as a sacrifice for the safety of the East. From the beginning of his reign Justinian turned his ambitions and gaze toward the West—toward the past. He expended enormous effort in order to revive that part of the empire which was dead, thus exhausting what was still alive.

Anastasius died in 518 without offspring and without naming a successor. The Senate and the army agreed that the throne should go to Justin, an uneducated Illyrian officer but a fine soldier. He was assisted and advised by his nephew Justinian, also Illyrian but with a solid classical background.

Although Justinian was not officially associated in the government of the empire until 527, it is generally considered that he was in charge after 518. His death was in 565, but nonetheless, because of the length of his reign, the sixth century deserves to be called the Century of Justinian.

Contemporaries have left us with pictures of him that are not always in agreement; yet all speak of his exceptional energy for work, which allowed him to manage all affairs himself. It caused him to be nicknamed by his exhausted colleagues "the emperor who never sleeps." He was also tremendously authoritarian and arrogant, very greedy for fame, pomp and the prestige due to an emperor. Finally, as goes without saying, he was very devout and well versed in theology. The part taken in government by the empress Theodora, with whom Justinian was passionately in love, is well known. She was crowned with him in 527. The daughter of a bear-keeper at the circus, she had once been a dancer and an actress; though her morals had been reputedly somewhat loose, after she came to the throne she was above reproach and gave herself entirely to her great task. She is no better portrayed than by the words she is said to have pronounced on the day of a terrible riot, known as the "Nika Insurrection," that almost overthrew Justinian. The latter was on the point of flight when Theodora stopped him with the often-quoted words: "When the only safety lies in flight, I would not flee. Those who wear the crown should not survive its loss. I like the old proverb: 'Purple is a beautiful shroud.'"

Justinian had two ideas and two aims. As a Roman emperor, he wished to re-establish the empire in its entirety and to restore its prosperity. As a Christian emperor, he believed it was right to impose a single orthodoxy on all, and to make authoritative decisions about the doctrines and organization of the Church. This explains his whole policy. His foreign policy can be entirely explained by his plan to reconquer the West, while his legislative and administrative work was devised to restore to the empire its original form and splendor. For a model, Justinian had the glorious Roman past. But Rome had no solutions to offer on religious questions; Justinian was in a quandary. He himself favored an understanding with the papacy and the West, but Theodora, perhaps more clear-sighted, and understanding better the importance of the provinces in the East, advised a policy favorable to Monophysitism.

Foreign Policy

Justinian's principal aim was to remake the Roman Empire; the main steps toward this were clear. To be able to move freely in the West, Justinian hurriedly terminated the Persian war. Then he recovered Africa from the Vandals, Italy from the Ostrogoths, and part of Spain from the Visigoths. Although he by no means reached the old frontiers of the Roman Empire, at least the Mediterranean became once more a Roman lake. But the Orient was awake: another Persian war, then invasions by the Huns and Slavs, threatened the empire. Caught on the defensive, Justinian could fight no longer and agreed to pay tribute. By skillful diplomacy he contented himself with keeping the barbarians at a distance. And at the same time, by a clever system of large fortifications on every frontier, he transformed the empire into "a vast fortified camp" (Charles Diehl).

Conquests in the West. As with the German problem, the Roman Empire had never known how to solve the problem of the Persians. Trajan's enormous effort had been in vain. Julian died fighting them, and his successor, Jovian, gave up the left bank of the Tigris. The campaign conducted by one of Justinian's best generals, Belisarius, from 527 to 531, was not decisive. Impatient to conclude the war, Justinian, in spite of its harsh terms, signed an "eternal peace treaty" in 532 with the new king, Chosroes; this could only be a respite. Justinian turned his attention immediately to the West.

The reconquest of the West, long hoped for by the Roman and orthodox population, which bore with reluctance the rule of Arian barbarians, began with the Vandal kingdom of Genseric in Africa. The pretext was the usurpation of Gelimer in 531. Belisarius opened a brilliant campaign in 533; by the following year Gelimer had been compelled to capitulate. The revolts of the Berbers should perhaps be considered a factor contributory to the victory. Belisarius' successor in Africa, Salomon, was defeated and killed, but order was finally established by John Troglita in 548. With the exception of Western Morocco, North Africa was again Roman.

The campaign against the Ostrogoths was longer and more difficult. It began immediately after the African victory in 535, the pretext chosen being the assassination of Amalasontha, the daughter and successor of Theodoric the Great, by her husband Theodat. The beginnings were brilliant: as well as Dalmatia, Belisarius conquered Sicily, Naples, Rome and Ravenna, the capital of the Ostrogoths. In 540 he brought the Ostrogoth king, Vitigus, in captivity to Constantinople and set him at the feet of Justinian. But all was thrown in the balance again by the energetic resistance of a new Gothic king, Totila. Belisarius, at the head of an army of inadequate size, was defeated. However, his successor, Narses, was more fortunate, and after a protracted and well-conducted campaign achieved a decisive victory in 552.

Finally, through a series of successful campaigns against the Visigoths, Justinian was able to conquer Southeast Spain. The emperor took numerous measures designed to restore to the territories he had conquered their ancient administrative organization. He divided them into two prefectures, Italy and Africa. But he was unable to realize more than a part of his projects: West Africa, three-quarters of Spain, and the whole of Gaul, including Provence, Noricum and Rhaetia (the defenses of Italy), still eluded him. Moreover, the territory that had been conquered was in a state of economic misery: the military forces that occupied it were insufficient. On the frontiers the barbarians were driven back but not crushed, and they continued to be a threat.

Dangers in the East.   These incomplete and precarious settlements had nonetheless cost the empire considerable effort. This becomes obvious when we see how Chosroes profited from the fact that Justinian had exhausted himself in the West. Chosroes chose this time to denounce the "eternal peace treaty" of 532. The Persians were temporarily victorious; in spite of the efforts of Belisarius they blazed a trail as far as the Mediterranean, ravaging Syria and sacking Antioch in 540. By paying two thousand pounds of gold each year, Justinian managed to buy respite on several occasions; and in 562 a fifty-year peace treaty was finally signed. Justinian pledged payment of large-scale tribute to the Persians and promised not to spread Christian propaganda in their lands. For their part, the Persians gave up territory that had long been the subject of dispute with the Romans: the country of the Lazes (ancient Colchis) on the east coast of the Black

Sea. Nor did they continue to occupy land on the Mediterranean or the Black Sea, where their presence had been
equally dangerous to Byzantium.

But danger immediately arose on the Danube frontier,
in the shape of the Huns and the Slavs. The former were in
the habit of crossing the Danube periodically and infiltrating
into Thrace. From there they made sallies into Greece, ravaging the land and casting their eyes on Constantinople and the
East. In the end they were always driven back over the frontiers, but the raids wore the countryside out.

Even more troublesome were the Slavs. Under Anastasius their bands had scored some points against the empire,
but it was under Justinian that the Slavic danger, thenceforth
an inseparable part of the history of Byzantium, first revealed
itself in all its seriousness. The more or less conscious object
of the Slavs was to acquire access to the Mediterranean. The
town they first chose for attack was Thessalonica, which, under Justinian, was on the point of becoming the second city
of the empire. Almost every year hordes of Slavs crossed the
Danube and made inroads into Byzantine territory. In Greece
they got as far as the Peloponnesus; in Thrace they reached
the villages on the outskirts of Byzantium; in the West they
reached the Adriatic. They were always driven back by Byzantine generals, but never crushed, coming back again the
following year in greater numbers. The age of Justinian "laid
the foundations for a Slavic problem in the Balkans" (A. Vasiliev).

Defense of the Empire. With incomplete conquest in
the West and difficult defenses in the East, the empire would
obviously have been unwise to rely on the strength of its army
alone. Although the army contained some admirable units,

particularly cavalry, it was not large enough; it has been estimated at only 150,000 men. Moreover it was far from homogeneous, since it contained a large proportion of barbarians as a result of peace treaties. Finally, it had the faults of all mercenary armies: it was undisciplined and greedy for plunder.

In order to lessen the demands on his army, Justinian covered the empire with fortifications. This was one of the biggest and most useful achievements of the reign, and it astonished and amazed the historian Procopius: in his tract *Historical Buildings* he enumerates the military fortifications of Justinian, and remarks that if he had not seen them with his own eyes he could hardly have conceived them to be the work of one man. In every province Justinian repaired or constructed buildings in their hundreds, from fortresses to the simplest of castles. These were naturally more numerous on the borders, where they formed several lines of defense stretching back a long way from the frontier. Every strategic point was guarded, every town of any importance protected. The barbarian hordes, even if they were still able to lay waste the countryside, which they often did, were forced to skirt these places, not knowing how to capture them. Thus they were unable to keep a hold on the ground they had won.

This wise organizing was completed by skillful diplomacy, justly called "the science of governing barbarians." This diplomacy exploited the barbarians' natural vanity and the prestige that the empire and the emperor had in their eyes; it included the generous bestowal on their leaders, after ceremonial reception at the Byzantine court, of honorary titles and offices. It encouraged evangelism also in barbarian countries, Byzantine influence penetrating to these concurrently with Christianity. From the eastern banks of the Black Sea to Abyssinia, Christian missions were numerous and generally effective. Finally, the policy made widespread use of loans and tribute.

This last process disclosed to Byzantium the weakness of the others. Procopius observed that it was futile to ruin the treasury by paying indemnities when the only effect was to make the recipients anxious for more. However, it was the inevitable consequence of Justinian's initial error. In the West he had wasted his strength in obtaining results that were illusory. These had been bought too dearly: the price was the uneasy and defensive attitude the empire was forced to adopt in the Orient.

Internal Achievement

Legislation.   Believing that his reconstruction of the empire would last, Justinian wanted to give it the order, prosperity and good government that he considered had been Rome's in its heyday. The measures he took can be divided into two categories: legislation and administrative reform.

Rome had founded a legal science through which the state had been given order and unity and the emperor the basis of his absolute power. Justinian understood the importance of this inheritance, the role it could still play and the necessity to keep it safe. Because he had this particular point of view, and sufficient determination to complete the task successfully, because he was able to enlist supporters capable of carrying out his designs, the legislation of Justinian has become the most celebrated and indeed the most remarkable part of his achievement.

What later came to be called the *Corpus Juris Civilis*

(the civil code) was made up of four sections: the *Code of Justinian*, as it should be called, a compilation of all the imperial constitutions from the time of Hadrian to the year 534; the *Digests* or *Pandects*, a synthesis of the work of the great legal experts, and a summary of the whole Roman jurisprudence; the *Institutes*, a practical manual of law for the use of students; and the *Novels*, the 154 ordinances published by Justinian after 534. It is interesting to note that the *Code*, the *Pandects* and the *Institutes* are in Latin, while most of the *Novels* are written in Greek, so that, as Justinian himself said, they would be understood by all. The concession cost the emperor a great deal, for he was no lover of Hellenism and only used the Greek language with reluctance.

One cannot overstress the importance of this work, first for Byzantium, which was assimilating what had been most worthwhile in Rome's civilizing mission, and secondly for the history of humanity. It is on Justinian law, often taken up as it stood, that the basis of much of the modern civil code rests. At the beginning of the twelfth century the West adopted it again as the guiding principle of social life and of the functioning of the state.

Administrative Reform.   In the strict sense the administrative reform of Justinian is principally contained in two ordinances of the year 535, by which the emperor gave his officials the outlines of his policy. In the broad sense his reform consisted of the whole wealth of measures that he took to improve life within the empire.

There was need for reform: the common people were greatly dissatisfied with the state officials and with the whole policy of the emperor in general. This was brought home to Justinian quite strongly by the terrible Nika insurrection in

Constantinople in 532, which received its name from its rallying cry—the Greek *nika*, victory, or "let us conquer." It broke out among the populace, who, as in all other great cities, were grouped together in districts (*demes*) in which political parties still held sway. Demonstration at the Hippodrome was the only way in which public opinion could vent its feelings; it was a kind of institution. When the emperor himself wished to speak to the people, he did it in this Circus from his high box. (Historians have recorded for us the rather curious dialogues that passed, in difficult times, between the emperor's spokesmen and the various factions.) The uprising of 532 began in the Circus and then spread through the whole city. The people were masters of Constantinople for six days, pillaging and burning. Even the promise of the dismissal of the two ministers most hated for the harshness of their rule, Tribonian and John of Cappadocia, was not enough to pacify them. It took Belisarius' strategy: he shut the rebels up in the Hippodrome and massacred at least 30,000 of them. The carnage extinguished the uprising but Justinian had learned his lesson.

The two ordinances of 535 were supplemented in the following years by more detailed measures, whose aim was to reform the official hierarchy. Unnecessary posts were eliminated, bribery in high places was suppressed and salaries were increased. Those entering office were now obliged to swear an oath, and certain special agents, or "justinians," were chosen in whom civil and military powers were united. All these measures were designed to make officials both more independent of those they administered and more dependent on the central government. Justinian also made pressing appeals for fairness (at the same time reforming the administration of justice), equity, honesty and benevolence.

Another series of measures was perhaps still more significant: those by which Justinian tried to remedy the injustices caused by the powerful entrenched landowners. He was aware that his opponents were proud of their landed aristocratic privileges and never deferred to the central government. In striking at them he struck at the same time at the most dangerous enemies of the middle class, the worst taxpayers, indeed the most serious threat to the prosperity of the state.

Justinian's insight was correct in attacking dishonest officials and rebellious landowners. But the result of his efforts was a failure for which the emperor was principally responsible. His constant and ever-increasing need for money resulted in he himself setting an example of bad administration and infringement of his own laws. Justinian's expenses for war, and above all for his great public works, were enormous. Hardly had he, in one ordinance, taken the side of the taxpayer crushed by tax authorities than in the next he empowered his tax-collectors to bring in as much money as possible by any means. Justinian put public offices up for sale, created new taxes and duties, and debased the currency. Officials were made personally responsible for the recovery of taxes, which policy opened the way to all the excesses so recently strongly condemned. Once again the official was merely a pitiless or dishonest tax-collector, and the taxpayer, to escape this scourge, hastened to swell the ranks of the clientele of the great landowners whom Justinian had wanted to humble.

Religious Policy. His concept of the "Roman Empire" and his Western policy naturally made an understanding with the papacy seem inviting to Justinian. This had seemed to be in the offing from the succession of Justin in 518. Under Justinian's influence the emperor was reconciled with Rome and

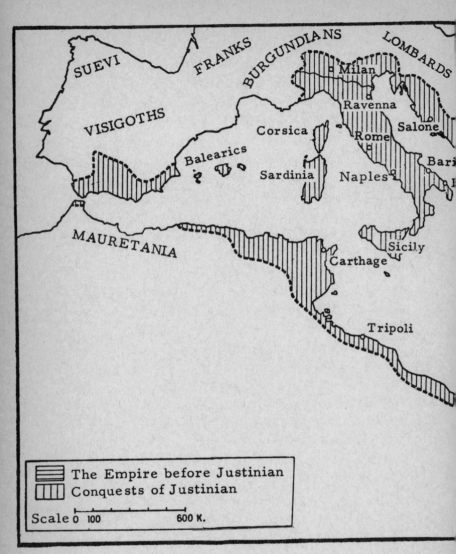

SUEVI

FRANKS

BURGUNDIANS

LOMBARDS

VISIGOTHS

Milan

Ravenna

Corsica

Salone

Rome

Balearics

Sardinia

Naples

Bari

MAURETANIA

Sicily

Carthage

Tripoli

The Empire before Justinian
Conquests of Justinian

Scale 0 100   600 K.

The Empire

of Justinian

the schism of Acacius came to an end. The emperor accepted the conditions of the pope and agreed to exclude from the Church's prayers Acacius and his successors, as well as the two emperors with Monophysitic leanings, Zeno and Anastasius. In the first two years of his personal rule (527 and 528) Justinian promulgated the most severe ordinances against heretics, almost making them outlaws. In 529 he ordered the closing of the University of Athens, the last refuge of paganism. His conquests in the West brought persecutions against the Arians and numerous protestations of deference to the papacy.

However, the empress Theodora was not, like the emperor, dazzled by the mirage of the West. She knew that the empire was, in the last analysis, a thing of the East and that the provinces of the Orient gave it its strength. Egypt and Syria in particular, the richest imperial provinces, were resolutely Monophysitic. For political reasons as well as from conviction, Theodora was throughout her life an advocate for the Monophysites. Enlightened by her, Justinian made decrees of tolerance on their behalf, accepted their representatives at Constantinople, and, in 535, permitted the bishop Anthimius, who had been converted to Monophysitism, to ascend the patriarchal throne. The response of Pope Agapetus was not long in coming: Anthimius was deposed, and an anathema was pronounced against Monophysites in 536 by the Council of Constantinople. The pope got Justinian to promise that he would execute these decisions, and terrible persecution swooped down on the Monophysites, even in Egypt.

Theodora had her revenge. In spite of the executions and the terrible measures taken, the heresy lived on. Its leaders were in Constantinople, in the palace of the empress herself.

Enthusiastic propaganda (to which the emperor shut his eyes) reconstructed throughout the Orient the communities that had been dispersed. In 543 Justinian went as far as to condemn at the so-called Council of the Three Chapters the texts that the Council of Chalcedon had approved, which was in a sense to compromise the authority of the latter council. To obtain the agreement of Pope Vigilus by permission or by force, Justinian compelled him to leave Rome and come to Constantinople; there, by dint of pleas and threats, he extracted from him a declaration confirming the decision of the Council of the Three Chapters.

The Monophysites seemed to have triumphed. But in the same year, 548, the empress Theodora died. Concurrently the whole of the West protested against the weakness of the pope, and he went back on his decision. Justinian took a strong line with Vigilus, had a fresh council condemn the texts already censured by the Three Chapters, and attempted to apply these decisions by force. But he only succeeded in causing a split in the West between those who rallied to his views and those who remained adamant. Moreover, this was done without giving satisfaction to the demands of the Monophysites in the East.

The failure was complete and his Western policy was once again the principal factor. Because of this the empire had been left helpless in the face of enemies who attacked the Orient. Because of this, the imperial finances had been exhausted and, consequentially, the administrative reforms wrecked. Because of this the last opportunity had been lost of giving the Christian East the religious unity it was to need so badly a century later when confronted by the Arab invasion.

Economic Life. Only the new aspects need be mentioned. One of the most important (and equally important from the social point of view) was the considerable development of monasticism. Justinian and Theodora cultivated it, emulating with sincere admiration the hermits of Egypt and Palestine. It was to become one of the most permanent characteristics of the Byzantine state, and to bring attendant dangers in its wake. For the monks had too much freedom of action and too important a place in the political life of the country, and even of the court. They were too numerous, and were often merely recruits avoiding conscription. They amassed considerable wealth through gifts that often escaped taxation. Land tended to pass into their hands. Alongside the great estates of the aristocracy was growing up a new kind of privileged property owner.

Another characteristic of Justinian's economy, at least in the early years, was the quantity and importance of large-scale public works: roads, bridges, fortifications, aqueducts and churches spread out over the entire empire. For some time, though at enormous cost, there appeared to be considerable prosperity. Then financial difficulties put a stop to this optimism and heavy taxation again oppressed the population.

As far as trade was concerned, Justinian's policy encouraged remarkable economic activity in certain privileged centers like Constantinople, where commercial exchange between East and West occurred. But the real problem the empire faced was that of relations with the Far East. The problem was how to facilitate the procurement of the products of India and China, especially silk. These were either brought by land as far as Sogdiana[1] or by sea to Ceylon,

---

[1] A district between the Jaxartes and Oxus rivers in Asia Minor.

where they were received and transported by the Persians to the Byzantine frontier. Justinian, trying to avoid the expensive and cumbersome Persian middle stage, sought a northern route by way of the Caspian and Black seas that would skirt Persia. He had no success. He looked southward, attempting to encourage the Christian populations of the Yemen and Abyssinia to reach India and China directly, but again failed. The empire was unable to shake off the economic dictates of Persia.

The Age of Justinian. Was Justinian's legislation, then, the sole defense that can be pleaded before history for an emperor who has nonetheless received the epithet "the Great"? It would be wrong to forget that Justinian had a truly imperial aura of grandeur about him. His acts were, for his time, sufficiently far-reaching for the civilization of the sixth century (one of the most brilliant periods in the history of Byzantium) to be called "The Age of Justinian." His powerful personality, his own initiative as emperor, is found not only in the whole sphere of intellectual life but also in the number of fine monuments that have been preserved in almost every part of the empire. We shall give only two examples.

At Ravenna it is enough to mention the churches of S. Vitale and of S. Apollinare Nuovo, where are preserved the most beautiful mosaics of the sixth century. All the majesty and brilliance of the imperial court under Justinian live for us in the magnificent compositions of S. Vitale, which show the emperor and the empress surrounded by the great figures of their retinue.

At Constantinople, too, Justinian's works were numerous: one above all has survived almost intact to the present day, and has become the symbol of the entire reign: Santa Sophia. Constantine's original basilica had been destroyed in 532 during the Nika insurrection. Justinian decided that in reconstructing it he would give it proportions and magnificence never yet attained and make the new church the cathedral of the empire. Two Greek architects from Asia Minor, Anthemius of Tralles[2] and Isidore of Miletus, were called in. Using a plan taken from that of the basilica, they succeeded in building a cupola no less than 107 feet across and 175 feet high. The emperor devoted enormous sums of money to its decoration, sculpture, paving, marble facings and mosaics. On the day of its solemn dedication, December 25, 537, which marks in a sense the climax of his reign, it is said that Justinian, on entering the cathedral, was seized with excitement and cried out, alluding to the great temple of Jerusalem: "I have surpassed you, Solomon!" Throughout the Middle Ages the basilica was usually called the Great Church, which was enough to distinguish it from all others. It is the masterpiece and at the same time the synthesis of the imperial art of the sixth century; it makes a harmony of elements borrowed from Rome, Greece, the Orient and Christendom.

Even if Justinian was often wrong—and his reign can be considered a protracted error—it should be recognized that it was not without grandeur: it is from Justinian that we must date Byzantine civilization proper.

Justinian's Successors. Justinian died in 565. His administration, always short of money, had been so oppressive, and exhaustion and misery were so great, that his death was welcomed with relief. The period that followed saw the suc-

[2] Modern Aidin Guzel-Hissr.

cession to the throne of Justin II (565-578), Tiberius (578-582), Maurice (582-602) and Phocas (602-610); it revealed harshly all the artificiality and excess in Justinian's work.

In foreign policy this period saw the abandonment of the plans in the West: Italy was almost entirely conquered by a new people, the Lombards. Rome, forsaken, found its only support in the energy of Pope Gregory the Great. To save what he still could, Maurice created the exarchies of Ravenna in Italy and Carthage in Africa, in which civil and military power were vested in the hands of one official, the exarch.

In the Orient war was rekindled on the Persian and Danube frontiers. The Persian war, so disastrous for the empire under Justin, was brought to a conclusion under Maurice with a treaty advantageous to Byzantium. But it was to start again under Phocas. The Danube frontier was continually violated by bands of Slavs assisted by a people of supposedly Turkish origin, the Avars. The Slavs made unsuccessful attacks on Thessalonica, laying waste the whole of the surrounding district and coming down as far as the Peloponnesus. Some doubtless settled there, and this has given credence to the famous outlandish theory of Jakob Fallmerayer that all Greeks had become "Slavicized" by about the turn of the sixth century.

Internal administration continued to be dominated by financial problems, which no emperor seemed able to solve. The death of Justinian was followed by a violent reaction against absolute monarchy both in Constantinople, where gangs terrorized the city, and in the provinces, where the landed aristocracy was restless.

In the field of religion, opposition indicative of the unrest of the time broke out suddenly between Pope Gregory the

Great and John the Ascetic, Patriarch of Constantinople, the latter having pretended to the title of "Universal Patriarch."

The period ended in the scandalous reign of Phocas, a junior officer swept onto the throne by popular and military support. Though he governed like a bloodthirsty tyrant he was ineffective, being unable to prevent the Persian armies from coming within sight of Constantinople. When Heraclius, the son of the Exarch of Carthage, arrived under the walls of the capital with a small fleet in 610, the same people who had made Phocas emperor put him to death and gave the throne to Heraclius.

4 / THE DYNASTY OF HERACLIUS AND THE END OF THE ROMAN EMPIRE (610-717)

General Characteristics

Heraclius ascended the throne in 610 and continued to reign until 641. His successors governed the empire until 717. Among these only two or three are worthy of mention, either for the length of their rule or the importance of their work: Constant II (642-668), Constantine IV (668-685) and Justinian II, called "the Broken-Nosed" (685-695 and 705-711).

According to Charles Diehl, the seventh century was one of the most gloomy periods in Byzantine history. It was an era of serious crisis, a decisive moment when the very existence of the empire seemed to hang in the balance. Another historian of Byzantium, George Ostrogorsky, considers Heraclius' epoch particularly important: he actually makes it the starting point for Byzantine history proper, since until then the empire, having territory in the West, could still be called Roman.

These views are well justified. In the seventh century

Byzantine civilization underwent an undeniable eclipse: there was an absence of writers, historians and great monuments; everywhere there was fear and the most crass superstition. This was not a sign of a lasting decline, but of a deep crisis that was to transform the face of the empire. Its origin lay in the lack of unity that set the West in opposition to the East. Even in the East itself, there were provinces that were orthodox and others that were Monophysitic. Justinian had failed in his exhausting effort to revive the spirit of Rome; the price of his misdirected ambition was the conquest by the Arabs in the following century of the richest provinces of the East, the lasting presence of the Slavs, and the creation of a Bulgar state.

Consequently, from all points of view—geographic, ethnic, economic, religious and administrative—the empire underwent a decisive transformation. It was no longer a Roman Empire, but rather a Greek Empire of the East. By adapting itself to these new conditions it survived, admittedly reduced in scale, but more homogeneous, better proportioned to its actual strength, and better prepared for the struggle against the enemies that were encircling it. In this form it was to last until the fifteenth century.

The Decline of Persia

Up till this period the two great world powers had been the Roman and Persian empires. The former now won a brilliant victory over the latter, before being vanquished in its turn by the Arabs.

In the first years of Heraclius' reign the Persians were more threatening than ever; their ephemeral conquests were the prelude to those the Arabs were soon to make. In 612 the

Persians were at Antioch; in 614, at Jerusalem (where they seized the most precious relics, notably part of the cross of Christ); in 618 or 619 they had reached Alexandria. Assisted by Sergius, the energetic Patriarch of Constantinople, who put at his disposal the wealth of the Church, Heraclius raised an army in Asia Minor and took the offensive in 622. A brilliant campaign (which later Western chroniclers tried to present as a forerunner of the Crusades) brought Heraclius into Armenia in 625, to Nineveh in 627, and into the heart of Persia in 628, the year of the death of Chosroes II. Heraclius dictated conditions of peace. The terms were that the Persians should give back all their conquests. In 629 the emperor was received in triumph at Constantinople, after which he took back to Jerusalem a relic that was declared to be a part of the Holy Cross.

As a result of internal decadence rather than of the victory of the Byzantines, Persia entered into a period of decline —hastened by Arab conquests—from which she never recovered. As a result Heraclius officially took the title of *Basileus,* which was the Greek name given to the King of Persia.

The Settlement of the Slavs in Greece

During the campaign in Persia in 626 the Avars besieged Constantinople, but the walls held fast and they were forced to retire. This success was attributed by the Byzantines to the protection of the Virgin, whose sanctuary on the outskirts of the city at Balchernae remained intact in the midst of the devastation. This setback and the subsequent decline of the Avar Empire resulted in another migration of the Slavs, who had for a long time been putting pressure on the Balkan frontier. Croats and Serbs settled in the northwest of the peninsula, spreading from there over all Illyricum. However, they became Christian and were for some time loyal vassals of the empire. But Slavonic tribes in ever-increasing numbers penetrated south of the Danube into Moesia, Thrace and Macedonia. Thessalonica was threatened several times and besieged in 617 and 619. The safety of the town on these occasions was attributed to the intervention of its patron saint, Demetrius.

Slavonic penetration took on a new characteristic: no longer simple raids, but the settlement of entire tribes in Greek territory. Communities of Slavs were formed, and in time almost the whole country became "Slavicized" while being repopulated. These communities were particularly numerous in Macedonia around Thessalonica, but there were also some in Epirus, Thessaly, Central Greece and the Peloponnesus. Some even got as far as the islands, traveling by boats made from a single tree trunk (*monoxyles*). For a long time relations between the empire and these undisciplined and ever-encroaching tribes were strained. Indeed, Constant II and Justinian II conducted military campaigns against them. But later friendly relations were established once again. In Macedonia the Slavs remained the dominant element and the empire had to put up with them, restricting itself to keeping a kind of indirect sovereignty over them. In the rest of Greece it seems certain that they were gradually Hellenized —though it is nevertheless true that the Balkan Peninsula was seriously disturbed from the ethnic point of view.

The Beginnings of Bulgaria

Much more serious for the future was the setting up of a Bulgar state between the Danube and the chain of the Hemus Mountains, toward the end of the seventh century. The ancient Bulgars were a people of Finno-Ugric origin who in the sixth century were making their presence felt in the Danube regions. In the seventh century they crossed the mouth of the Danube and settled in what is now Dobrudja. In 679 Constantine IV started a campaign against these newcomers, but he was defeated and undertook to pay them tribute. Under the terms of the treaty, he abandoned to them territories south of the lower Danube. From this beginning the Bulgars progressively extended their authority at the expense of the Slavonic tribes who had preceded them in these regions. On the one hand, the Bulgars, numerically inferior, became so Slavic that they even forgot their mother tongue; on the other, the Slavs, up to then extremely dispersed, suffered the rigorous political yoke that the Bulgars imposed on them. The result of all this was the establishment of a state in northern Thrace that was soon to be very powerful, and that, in the following centuries, played in the life of the empire a role as important as it was sinister. It is significant that the empire was in fact abandoning its ancient frontier on the Danube, which had so long protected it, and was falling back to the mountains north of Thrace.

The Arab Conquests

But the great event of the seventh century—and not only for the Byzantine Empire, which was its principal victim—was the Arab conquest.

This is no place to expound the origins of Islam, or even explain the rapidity of its military success. Some theories point to the desperate energy the Arabs drew from their very poverty and misery, or again, to the aggressive zeal inherent in their religious fanaticism. The numerical weakness and poor quality of the Byzantine army, and the feeble state of

Byzantine administration in the provinces, were much more important. But the decisive point was the lack of skill that Byzantium showed in its religious policy, particularly toward the Monophysites, whom Justinian's successors continued to combat. Heraclius' attempts at union, and the new doctrine of Monothelitism[1] that he created expressly to bring orthodoxy and Monophysitism closer together, failed completely. Monothelitism was rejected with equal horror by both sides. There was obviously no possible agreement. The Monophysitic provinces—Egypt, Syria and Palestine—had reached the point where they wanted to be separated from Byzantium; they preferred the domination of the Arabs, who at least were known for their spirit of tolerance.

In the last years of his reign the Arabs relieved Heraclius of those provinces he had won back from the Persians. In 634 they took Basra; in 635, Damascus; and in 636, at the battle of Yarmuk, the Byzantines suffered a disaster that marked their final loss of Syria. In 637 or 638 the Arabs captured Jerusalem, and Palestine fell. In 639 they pushed on as far as Mesopotamia; and in 641 or 642 they captured Alexandria, and Egypt was theirs. It was the turn of Cyrenaica and Tripoli next, then Cyprus and Rhodes. Finally they attacked Constantinople.

These attacks on Constantinople by land and sea were repeated five years in succession from 673 to 677. Constantine IV withstood them energetically, one of the main factors in his success being his use of Greek fire.[2] In 677 the Arab fleet

[1] A doctrine recognizing in Christ one Will and two Natures.
[2] The name applied to inflammable and destructive compositions used in warfare in the Middle Ages. The Byzantines probably used a mixture of sulphur, naphtha and quicklime that ignited spontaneously when wetted.

left Constantinople, but on its way back to Syria it ran into a violent storm a long way off the south coast of Asia Minor; the damage it suffered turned to disaster when the Byzantine fleet intervened. At the same time the Arabs were checked on land and signed a peace with the empire.

This seemed a great victory. Constantine IV's resistance, which fortunately put a stop to the astonishing progress of the Arabs, was of great consequence. But only a part of Asia Minor was left in his hands; Syria, Palestine, Egypt and a section of North Africa now belonged to the Arabs. The menace that burdened the West grew heavier: from 693 to 698 Byzantine Africa, including Carthage, passed entirely into Moslem hands.

The Themes and the Militarization of the Empire

These were the most serious upheavals experienced by the ancient world since the Roman conquests, if not those of Alexander. They had an immense effect on the internal organization of the empire in all domains. The empire's evolution toward a new administrative system, that of the *themes*, was hastened.

We have seen how separation of civil and military power was a principle of Roman administration for several centuries. But the system of the themes, on the contrary, rested on the concentration of both powers in the same hands—a measure that states have recourse to when seriously threatened. It is possible that Persia adopted it in the sixth century and that the Byzantine Empire followed its example. In any case the new organization was not created all at once, but progressively applied in provinces as they found themselves under attack. Already, under Justinian, certain regions had been placed under the authority of a Justinian praetor, or "count," who took on all powers. Under his successors, the West, threatened by Lombards and Moors, saw the creation of the two exarchies of Ravenna and Carthage; here in fact authority was entirely in the hands of the Exarch and the dukes. In the seventh century the system was expanded and soon received a new name. The Greek word *thema*, which originally meant an army corps, came to mean the district within which this unit operated. Because all power was concentrated in the hands of one military person—a general, the *strategus*—the theme came to replace the eparchy as the administrative subdivision of the empire.

Themes came into existence as they were needed. The Armenian theme was perhaps the first to be set up, the Anatolian one coming later: these were to protect Asia Minor from the Arab danger. Then came the theme of Opsikion for the defense of the capital itself. There was even a theme for the sea, in response to the threat of the Arab fleet; one in Thrace, as a counter to the Bulgars; and one in Greece, to control the Slavs. In Sicily the theme was designed to continue the struggle against the Arab threat in the West. It is obvious that the new organization, only completed in the eighth century, while upsetting provincial administration and the subdivisions of the empire, followed faithfully the steps dictated by external dangers.

The General Transformation of the Empire

The institution of themes was, however, only one of the profound changes that altered the image of the empire in the seventh and eighth centuries.

First of all, the empire changed geographically. In the

West there remained no more than a few possessions with their connections already almost severed and with little loyalty. In the East the empire had been reduced to Asia Minor and Greece. The losses in the West made the "Roman idea," to the degree that it survived, still more utopian. But to measure the importance of the damage suffered in the East, it is enough to recall the roles that Syria and Egypt had played for centuries: Beirut, Antioch and Alexandria had been the most prosperous ports in the Mediterranean; Syrian industry had been the most energetic; Egypt, after being the granary of Rome, had become the same for Byzantium. To this economic importance should be added the part played by the two provinces in the whole Byzantine civilization—in art, literature and theology. The Hellenism of Byzantium had long been more Syrian and Alexandrian than Asiatic. Byzantium was losing the most important part of its inheritance.

The result was sudden unbalance, made worse still by the fact that Greece was undergoing during this period a wholesale absorption of Slavic ideas that modified its character. From the beginning of the seventh century on, the Byzantine Empire consisted properly of Asia Minor. Indeed, the dynasty of Heraclius was probably Armenian. In the centuries that followed, more and more Asiatics occupied the throne. It is interesting to note also that Heraclius modified recruitment to the army in this direction. We have already seen what a great part barbarian recruitment played before his reign; Heraclius seems to have reverted to a policy of recruiting Byzantine citizens and looking for these in the Orient, where he had already raised the great army that defeated the Persians. It has been suggested, but without conclusive proof, that the emperors of the seventh century, to insure regular service, revived and extended the institution of soldier settlement. This had already existed previously for the army on the frontier: hereditary and inalienable land-holdings were granted to the families of soldiers in exchange for service.

The territorial losses experienced by the empire, though economically crippling, were compensated for by greater ethnic homogeneity. There was a similar result in the sphere of religion: in losing the Monophysitic provinces the empire lost the most obstinate opponents to a policy of conciliation with the West. The consequence of this was immediate: at the Council of Constantinople in 681 Constantine IV had Monothelitism condemned and orthodoxy restored. Another source of dispute also disappeared at the same time: the rivalries between the Patriarch of Constantinople on one hand, and those of Alexandria, Jerusalem and Antioch on the other. Thenceforth all Eastern Orthodoxy was firmly centered around the Patriarch of Constantinople, who became consequently more important, and whose influence over the government and the minds of the emperors increased. From then on throughout the history of Byzantium the ideas of orthodoxy and nationality were interlocked.

Finally, as a result of the same territorial and ethnic concentration, the empire acquired another characteristic: it was clearly becoming a Greek Empire, or if one prefers, a Greco-Asiatic one. The myth of a Roman Empire—which Justinian's efforts had for a century been able to preserve—was disappearing, together with the decline of the Latin language. Indeed the surest indication of this Hellenization was the triumph of Greek, confirmed in the seventh century. Henceforth Greek became the official language—the language of the ad-

ministration, the army and authority in general. Officials'
titles were Hellenized, even the imperial title itself.

5 / THE ISAURIAN AND AMORIAN DYNASTIES; ICONOCLASM (717-867)

The Emperors

The dynasty of Heraclius had ended in usurpation, anarchy and revolt. The last emperor, Theodosius III, incapable of restoring order, had abdicated when Leo, an Anatolian general, had himself crowned emperor in Santa Sophia at the instigation of his supporters.

Leo III reigned from 717 to 741. He is generally reckoned to have been an Isaurian, although he probably came from Germaniceia in northern Syria. He ruled jointly with his son Constantine V (Constantine Copronymus, 741-775), and the latter did the same with his son Leo IV (775-780). These three emperors form the Isaurian dynasty proper; they were responsible for more than sixty years of stable government for the empire.

Leo IV took as his wife an Athenian, Irene. On her widowhood she herself governed from 780 to 797, at first as regent for her son Constantine VI; then, when he reached his majority, she had him blinded and deposed, and continued to reign from 797 to 802 alone. She was the first woman who was in the real sense Empress of Byzantium.

Irene was deposed by her Minister of Finance, Nicephorus I, who was perhaps of Arab stock (802-811). He perished in a war against the Bulgars, and then, after two rather troubled years, the throne went to the *strategus* of Anatolia, Leo V (813-820), who was assassinated. The accession of a commander of the guard, Michael II (820-829), from Amorium in Phrygia, known as "the Stammerer," marks the beginning of the Amorian dynasty, which includes Theophilus (829-842) and Michael III, "the Drunkard" (842-867). But for the first fourteen years of the reign of Michael III, the real ruler was his mother Theodora, who acted as regent She was followed by the emperor's uncle, Bardas. For a century and a half all the Byzantium emperors, with the exception of Irene the Athenian, were Asiatic.

Evaluation of this period is often contradictory. It was a logical consequence of the seventh century. In foreign relations, the Slav, Bulgar and Arab problems were essentially the same. The loss of the West and the coronation of Charlemagne were merely the consequences of the orientalization of the empire. Administratively, the system of the themes became established, setting in motion a process begun in the previous century. In legislation, the *Ecloga* reflected this orientalization by replacing Latin with Greek. In religion, iconoclasm seemed a particularly violent reaction to superstition, the practice of idolatry, and the excessive power of the monks—all consequences of the turmoil in the seventh century. However, the reaction was futile: the situation was almost the same in 867 as it had been in 717. Historically, the period of two and a half centuries forms a whole, running from the end of the century of Justinian to the advent of the Macedonian dynasty.

The Arabs

The greatest threat of all to the empire remained the Arabs. In the years of anarchy (711-717) they had made considerable progress. In 717 they set out from Pergamum and crossed the Hellespont: their vast army attacked Constantinople by land, and a fleet of considerable strength supported them by sea. The defense of the city was conducted extremely energetically by Leo III. He had the foresight to conclude an agreement with the Bulgars, who harassed the attacking Arab army. The Arabs' mettle was also severely tested by famine and the rigors of the winter of 717-718, and they soon retreated, making no further attempt on Constantinople. In later years Leo III, who had married his son Constantine to the daughter of the Khan of the Khazars, found in the latter a most effective ally against the Arabs. He himself at the end of his reign managed to defeat the Arab armies in Phrygia at the great battle of Acroinon, forcing them to evacuate the western part of Asia Minor.

The defeat of the Arabs by Byzantium had great reverberations and was an event of the utmost importance Leo III's success put an end to the Arab advance in the East, just as the victory of Charles Martel at Poitiers in 732 marked the end of the Arab offensive from Spain against the West. But under Irene the Arabs were again victorious, forcing the empire to accept a humiliating treaty. During the reign of Michael II they gave effective support to a rebel, Thomas the Slav, who kept Constantinople in a state of siege for a year.

Moslem warships also seized Crete, which became for a hundred and fifty years a hideout for pirates and an embarrassment to the empire. In 838, during Theophilus' reign, the Arabs seized Amorium, cradle of the dynasty; the emperor, losing his nerve, sought assistance from the Venetians and Louis the Pious in the West, but only obtained promises. Fortunately, a few years later, Bardas was to triumph at Poson in Mesopotamia. But in the West, Sicily revolted and appealed to the Arabs of North Africa. They responded promptly, conquering the island and going on to seize Tarentum and Bari as well.

The Bulgars and the Russians

Under Leo III the Bulgars and the empire were at peace. But Constantine V took on himself the task of destroying their growing power. Fully aware of the danger, and directing several campaigns himself, he was victorious at the great battle of Anchialus in 762. But in the end he failed, and under Irene the Bulgars forced the empire to pay them tribute. Nicephorus took up the struggle again, this time against the terrible Khan Krum; but he was defeated and killed, and Khan Krum had his skull made into a drinking-cup. In 813 Krum laid siege to Constantinople, creating enormous panic in the city. But he did not succeed in capturing it after all, and in the following year he was dead. His successor, Omortag, made peace with Leo V, and both of them solemnly set about to delimit the frontier of Thrace. Omortag's son, Malamir, who succeeded him in 831, invaded Macedonia but then signed a truce with Theodora. His nephew, Boris, who came to the throne in 852, was converted to Christianity and brought his people with him into the Church.

The empire, sometimes by force of arms, sometimes by diplomacy, and sometimes by religious propaganda, succeeded more or less in restraining the Bulgars. But the formidable threat of this empire in its full flower remained, and the fortifications erected in Thrace by Constantine V and Leo V were a feeble defense against its expanding power. Moreover, toward the end of the Amorian dynasty, another danger appeared for the first time: the Russians attacked Constantinople by sea. Michael III was in Asia at the time and the fleet was in the West, but the defense of the city was energetically conducted by the patriarch Photius, and the Russians were forced back in a disastrous retreat. It was the Russians' first appearance in history and it meant a new danger for Byzantium.

Iconoclasm

But the most important phenomenon of the period was iconoclasm. Derived from Greek, the word literally means "the destruction of images." The iconoclastic movement appears to have originally been a reaction against the adoration and worship of holy images; later it concentrated opposition on certain other practices judged superstitious, such as the lighting of candles and the burning of incense. Finally, it sometimes took the form of an attack on the worship of the Virgin and the saints, especially the cult of holy relics.

In 725 or 726 Leo III (who had written a letter to the pope in which, according to the best Byzantine tradition, he proclaimed himself "Emperor and Priest") issued the first edict against images. We do not know what was in the text, but we do know that its application provoked riots, notably in Constantinople, where the emperor's officers destroyed a famous image of Christ. A council held at Constantinople in 730 condemned images, while in the following year an opposition council in Rome proclaimed an anathema on those who objected to them. Constantine V was even more violently iconoclastic than Leo III, even condemning the worship of the Virgin and the saints. In 753 he called together in Constantinople another council that solemnly condemned images. This was followed by the destruction or whitewashing of icons and the breaking up of collections of relics. At the same time the emperor began an energetic struggle against the monks, naturally the most ardent defenders of images. He confiscated monastic property, turned the monasteries over to secular use, and sent the monks packing. Irene, however, was fiercely devoted to image-worship and submissive to the guidance of monks. At the seventh ecumenical council (which could not be held in 786 at Constantinople because of army opposition, but was held the following year at Nicaea), Irene had the worship of relics and images reinstated. The monks got back their monasteries, wealth and privileges, and never ceased their exaggerated adulation of the empress who, some years later, was to put out the eyes of her son.

The dispute about iconoclasm was rekindled after Irene. Nicephorus, though ostensibly tolerant, was nonetheless hostile to monks. He sent the celebrated abbot of the monastery of Studius at Constantinople into exile together with his most enthusiastic supporters. This abbot, Theodore, had been the spirited leader of the monastic and pro-icon party. Leo the Armenian, Michael the Stammerer and Theophilus were iconoclasts, vigorously enforcing the measures of their predecessors. But in 815 a council held in Santa Sophia came out in favor of a moderate form of iconoclasm. Then for a second time a woman re-established the worship of images: in 842 Theodora rescinded the iconoclastic laws forever, and at a second council held in 843 had the provisions of the second council of Nicaea in 787 renewed. On March 11, 843, a solemn ceremony took place in Santa Sophia to celebrate what was called "the restoration of orthodoxy"; the Greek church still commemorates this each year.

These are the facts. But what should be the interpretation? Iconoclasm seems to have had two aspects and two sources of origin: religious and political:

1. *The Religious Aspect.* Some people represent the iconoclastic emperors as free-thinkers before their time. On the contrary, they were men of profound belief, who for this very reason wished to purge the Christian religion of what appeared to them as a superstition close to paganism. The worship of images was in no way a part of early Christianity; purists had for a long time forbidden the depiction of sacred subjects inside churches. Nevertheless images were introduced under the influence of ancient tradition, because their value in edification and instruction was recognized. The process was carried to extremes: images were no longer seen as symbols, but rather the sanctity and miraculous power of the persons depicted were also attributed to their representations, and these were offered personal worship. The iconoclasts' struggle was against the abuses that this idolatry entailed, and against other similar excesses. Opposing them were the simple-minded, the superstitious, women, the populace, monks and a large part of the clergy. With the iconoclasts were the more enlightened sections of society, leading secular clerics naturally disturbed at the power of the monks, and a large section of the population of the central and eastern provinces of Asia Minor, who had long been opposed to im-

ages. Moreover, the army, which contained more and more recruits from these regions, was with them. Vasiliev was right to point out that the iconoclastic emperors were themselves Isaurians, Armenians and Phrygians.

The Political Aspect.   It is not necessary to believe that the iconoclastic emperors attempted to rally to the imperial cause devotees of the aniconic religions, like the Jews and the Arabs, or the Paulician sect, who were opposed both to images and to the worship of saints. This supposition seems rather unlikely. One is struck by the role the monastic problem played in this dispute. As has been seen above, the considerable increase in the number of monks and monasteries, and in their power, wealth and privileges, had become a danger; the monks constituted a state within a state. Because they were fully aware of this danger, with its political, economic and social repercussions, the iconoclastic emperors conducted a desperate struggle against the monks, forcing them to disperse and secularizing their property.

Thus the iconoclastic dispute ended by becoming a dispute between Church and State. At the height of the struggle the leaders of the monastic party, Plato, abbot of the monastery of Saccoudion in Bithynia, and above all his nephew, Theodore the Studite, asserted the independence of the Church from the State. The emperor was refused the right to intervene in questions of religion and dogma. This was the very doctrine of the West, and Theodore the Studite, who had been exiled by Nicephorus, was in fact appealing to the pope. The monks, on obtaining satisfaction on the question of the worship of images and on recovering their privileges, did not insist on the proclamation of the independence of the Church. Ultimately, nothing had changed.

But iconoclasm had had still further results, which demonstrated once again the intimate connection between religious and political problems in Byzantium. The most unexpected was the strengthening of Greek influence in the south of Italy, to which many monks had migrated. The most important was the further widening of the gulf between East and West and, doubtless, the hastening of the final cleavage between the two parts of the empire of Justinian. The papacy had in effect taken up a position against the iconoclasts. When Pope Stephen II was instructed by Constantine V to seek help against the Lombards from Pepin the Short, he turned traitor to the cause of the heretic emperor. In 754 he contrived to have recognized his personal right to administer the territories of Rome and Ravenna, which had been reconquered by Pepin. This meant the loss of Italy for the empire. In 774, when he had destroyed the kingdom of the Lombards, Charlemagne solemnly confirmed to the pope the gift of Pepin. The papacy had now lost its confidence in the Eastern Empire; henceforth it was looking for a protector in the West. The coronation of Charlemagne by the pope on Christmas Night, 800, and the creation of a Christian Empire in the West, were to some extent the consequences.

In the closing years of the period several religious events are significant. Eastern Christianity, scourged and somewhat invigorated by the struggles of iconoclasm, greatly extended its influence over the barbarians. In 863 Cyril and Methodius left Thessalonica on an evangelical mission to Moravia; they were to become the apostles of the Slavs. In 864 Boris, Tsar of the Bulgars, was baptized at Constantinople and took the Christian name of Michael; he thereupon forced baptism on his people also. However, mistrust and rivalry grew between Rome and Constantinople. When the caesar Bardas deposed

Patriarch Ignatius, a supporter of images, so as to give the patriarchal throne to Photius, Ignatius appealed to Pope Nicholas I. The latter took his part, excommunicating Photius in 863. Photius, linking his personal case with the national cause of Byzantium, pronounced an anathema on the pope and denounced his illegal intervention in the affairs of the Eastern church at a council in Constantinople in 867. This action has become known as the schism of Photius.

6 / THE MACEDONIAN DYNASTY AND THE IMPERIAL ZENITH (867-1081)

The Emperors

The period that we now enter is, together with, the century of Justinian, one of the two most glorious in the history of the empire. The victorious Byzantine armies contained or repulsed the onslaught of their various enemies and increased the extent of the empire. At the same time Byzantine civilization flowered into what has justly been called the second Golden Age. Not since Justinian had Byzantium enjoyed such great prestige, nor was it again to achieve such brilliant success. In the works of the great French Byzantine scholar, G. Schlumberger—*Nicephorus Phocas* and *The Byzantine Epic* —it has long been possible to read the history of that heroic era. It is only possible here to sketch in the general features of the period.

A most unusual fact comes to mind first: what was accomplished was not the work of a single individual—as in Justinian's time—but rather the achievement of a succession of emperors, all remarkable for different qualities. The dynasty was founded by Basil I, the descendant of an Armenian family whose home was in Macedonia. From this the dynasty receives its accepted but inexact title. Basil, thanks to his physical strength and his ability to school wild horses, became the favorite of the last of the Amorian emperors, Michael III. The latter took him in as his assistant in the running of the empire; then, in 866, Basil succeeded in arranging the assassination of the emperor's uncle, the caesar Bardas. In the following year the emperor, too, died at his command, and from 867 to 886 Basil reigned alone.

His sons, Leo VI ("the Wise") and Alexander, ruled from 886 to 913, Leo wielding the real power. In order to obtain a son for the succession, Leo contracted marriages with four women, one after another, causing a great scandal. Such determination seems remarkable and bears witness to the concern with legitimacy. Thenceforth there existed a royal imperial family, whose members were called *Porphyrogeniti* (the word refers to the fact that they were supposed to be born in a purple room in the palace). The son of Leo VI, Constantine VII (Constantine Porphyrogenitus), occupied the throne from 913 to 959. However, from 913 to 959 the government was in fact in the hands of a co-emperor, Romanus Lecapenus, who was of Armenian origin. Romanus II, the son of Constantine VII, reigned from 959 to 963. On his death, his widow, Theophano, married the general Nicephorus Phocas, the commander-in-chief in Asia Minor, who was later assassinated in 969.

His murderer, John Tzimisces, an Armenian by birth, reigned from 969 to 976, insuring the acceptance of his legitimacy as ruler by marrying Theodora, the daughter of Constantine Porphyrogenitus. On his death, the two sons of Romanus II—Basil II, called "the Bulgar-Slayer," and Constantine VIII (976-1028)—ruled jointly. At this juncture an unsettled period began and the dynasty went into decline. The most important figure was the empress Zoë, who became the wife of three successive emperors: Romanus III (Romanus Argyrus), Michael the Paphlagonian and Constantine Monomachus. For a time she actually governed the empire directly, with the help of her younger sister, Theodora—the last example of rule by women in the history of Byzantium.

It is a remarkable fact that the so-called Macedonian dynasty was actually Armenian: Romanus Lecapenus, who ruled for Constantine VII, was Armenian; so was John Tzimisces, the usurper. Another characteristic shared by these emperors was that they were soldiers first and foremost. The only notable exceptions were Leo VI and Constantine VII. But under Constantine VII, it was a Roman admiral, Lecapenus, who actually governed.

The Arabs in East and West

On all frontiers save that of the Danube, the empire was involved in a struggle with the Arabs. Basil I and Leo VI set out on campaigns almost every year, sometimes with success, but never winning a decisive victory. In the West they recaptured Tarentum; but to offset this the Arabs completed and consolidated their conquest of Sicily, taking Syracuse, Taormina and Reggio. In the Orient they pushed back eastward the imperial frontier in Asia Minor. But in 904 a band of Moslem pirates seized Thessalonica in a surprise attack, pillaged the town and made a rapid retreat back to Syria, carrying off a horde of loot and more than 20,000 prisoners.

This was the signal for an energetic reprisal. Under Romanus Lecapenus the empire had some success in Upper Mesopotamia, and Edessa was recaptured. Nicephorus Phocas and John Tzimisces, both as generals and later as emperors, achieved decisive victories. Phocas recaptured Crete and Cyprus, Tarsus and Cilicia, and more important, Aleppo and Antioch in Syria. Tzimisces took the war as far as the Euphrates, organizing what amounted to a crusade for the recovery of the holy places. He recaptured Damascus and part of Palestine, but did not reach Jerusalem. Basil II was able to hold these conquests but did not appreciably add to them. Nonetheless in three places—Crete, the Euphrates and Syria—the empire had achieved decisive results.

Gains were no less clear in Armenia, which had been one of the principal playthings in the never-ending contest between the Persian and Roman empires. The Arabs had occupied it in the seventh century. But in the ninth century the Armenian dynasty of the Bagratids was restored to the throne with the joint consent of the Arabs and the Byzantines, both of whom needed Armenian support. It was Byzantium that was to get the upper hand, when, under Romanus Lecapenus, her influence grew in Armenia. Then, during the reign of Basil II, a part of Armenia was conquered, and the rest made into a vassal state. Under Constantine Monomachus the capital, Ani, was taken and the Bagratid family once again deposed.

During these glorious reigns Byzantium in no way renounced her claim to Italy, where Leo VI was busy setting up the two themes, admittedly small in size, of Lombardy and Calabria, later to be replaced by the catepanate of Bari. It is even possible that he wished to take back from the emperor in the West the titles the latter had usurped. There appears to have been a dispute with Louis II about the imperial title, and perhaps also one with Otto, crowned in Rome in 962 and founder of the Holy Roman Empire. But the danger from the Arabs reduced these quarrels to matters of secondary importance. Phocas made overtures to Otto for an alliance against Islam, the occasion of the famous mission of Liudprand to Constantinople. As a result of this, Tzimisces gave the Byzantine princess Theophano in marriage to Otto II, who, moreover, had been beaten by the Arabs. But Basil II was victorious against the Turks at Cannes. In this battle we see the first sign of the Norman danger. Basil's success reaffirmed Byzantium's position in Italy, thus permitting Michael IV to fit out an expedition against the Arabs in Sicily during which George Maniakes recaptured Messina.

The Bulgarians and the Danube Frontier

The Bulgarian danger was more localized but far more serious than the danger from the Arabs. Conflict with the Bulgarians broke out during the reign of Boris' son and successor, Simeon, who had been brought up in Constantinople. In time-honored Byzantine diplomatic fashion Leo VI, so as to divert their threatening attacks from himself, appealed to the Magyars (or Hungarians); this marks their entry into history. They promptly invaded northern Bulgaria. Simeon, for his part, called in the Petchenegs, and with their assistance drove off the Magyar onslaught. Following this up, Simeon also defeated the Greeks and even got as far as the walls of Constantinople. Leo VI was obliged to sign a treaty and pay tribute.

At this point Simeon turned his attention to Thessalonica.

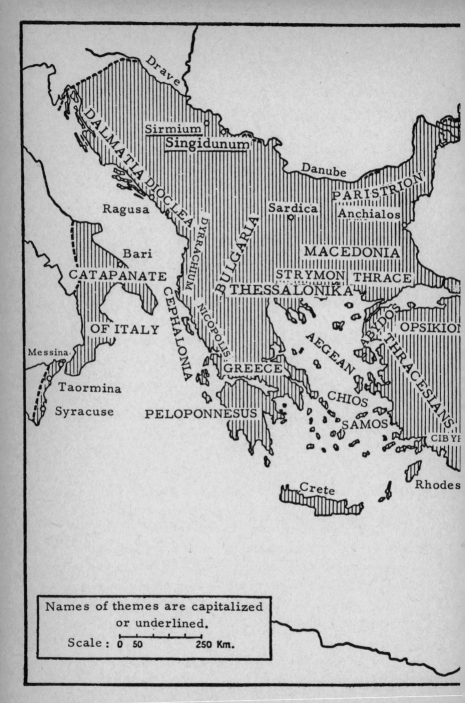

The Empire after the conquests

of the Macedonian emperors

In order to avoid surrendering it to him, Leo VI was obliged to cede vast tracts of land in southern Macedonia. But Simeon had as his final objective the capture of Constantinople; his intention was to become "Tsar of the Bulgars and Emperor of the Romans," a title that for a short time he did assume. In 922 he captured Adrianople. Ultimately all of Macedonia and Thrace except Thessalonica and Constantinople were his. He even laid siege to the capital. Once again the city believed it was lost, and once more it was saved by its fortified walls. It was probably at this time, about 924, that there took place a dramatic meeting on the walls of the city between Simeon and Romanus Lecapenus, the latter having spent the night praying in Santa Sophia. A truce was agreed upon, the sole condition being that the Byzantines should pay tribute in return for Simeon's withdrawal. What actually happened at the meeting is unknown, but it is often said that the Bulgarian tsar was impressed by the stature of the emperor of Byzantium. It seems more plausible that Simeon agreed to be conciliatory because he himself was under threat of attack from the Serbs; also, he had failed in his overtures to the Arabs for a joint operation to encircle Byzantium.

Simeon died in 927, and under his successor, Peter, Bulgaria experienced a rapid decline, hastened by internal friction. Nicephorus Phocas and John Tzimisces took up the struggle again, receiving help on one occasion from the Russians of Svjateslav. Eastern Bulgaria, if not all of it, was conquered by the Byzantines, and once again their armies reached the Danube frontier. The question came up again in subsequent years when Tsar Samuel reorganized the Bulgarian forces in western Bulgaria, reconstituting an empire that extended from the Danube to Thessaly and the Adriatic.

Basil II, who waged war against Samuel from 986 to 1014 with a savagery and ferocity equal to that of the Bulgars, richly deserves his title "the Bulgar-Slayer." The decisive battle took place in 1014 to the north of Serres: the Bulgarian army was completely overwhelmed and Basil took 15,000 prisoners. He had these blinded, sparing only one man in every hundred to act as guide when he sent the pathetic band back to Samuel. Some weeks later Samuel died and the whole of Bulgaria was conquered and put under a Byzantine governor. The empire was once again mistress of the entire Balkan Peninsula.

However, this did not bring complete security to the northern frontier of the Danube. Even if we do not mention the Magyars, who had been shown a route south, or the Petchenegs between the Danube and the Dnieper, who ultimately compelled Byzantium to pay tribute, there were the Russians. The latter became an increasingly serious danger. Tradition has it that Prince Oleg came on a military expedition to Constantinople in 907. Whether this expedition, said to have been followed by a treaty, is historical or legendary is controversial. But what is certain is that relations, both hostile and friendly, multiplied enormously between Byzantium and Russia. From the beginning of the tenth century there were important companies of Russian mercenaries in the Byzantine armies; and under Romanus Lecapenus, Constantinople was attacked twice by Prince Igor, in 941 and 944. A treaty was concluded and Igor left for Kiev. It was under Basil II that a true settlement was achieved: the emperor made an alliance with the Russian prince Vladimir, who was baptized and married a Byzantine princess. In 988 or 989 Vladimir had his own people baptized. This gives fresh proof of the skill with which Byzantium combined military strength, diplomatic ability and religious propaganda.

The Social Problem

In internal affairs the emperors were first and foremost concerned with the serious question of the laws governing land tenure. Documents of the period speak quite freely of the opposition between "men of status" and "the poor." The "men of status" were the large landowners, who, after the failure of the socialist revolution led by Thomas the Slav in the ninth century, achieved considerable influence. Indeed, on their own estates (often as large as whole provinces) they often took on the airs of independent petty kings. The poor were mostly small peasant landowners with tiny plots. Sometimes these had received their land as an emolument for their military service. The intimidation and threats of the great, and the excessive demands of the treasury on occasion, led these people to seek out protection and security by allying themselves with "men of status." For these benefits they often had to sacrifice their liberty. The disappearance of the small property owner had serious economic, fiscal and military consequences. The tremendous growth in power of the large landowners can be seen from the fact that, during the reign of Basil II, a revolt of two of them, Bardas Phocas and Bardas Skeleros, only just failed to unseat the emperor.

In 922, a new piece of legislation of Romanus Lecapenus began a series of measures aimed at remedying this state of affairs by making illegal the acquisition of poor men's property by men of status. It also gave preference to the peasant if he was in competition with a large landowner for the purchase of property. The legislation also enjoined that all sol-

diers' property seized or bought should be restored to its
rightful owners. These measures were reiterated by Romanus
Lecapenus in a new law of 934. Basil II showed himself particularly unsympathetic toward the rich: his law of 996 did
away with the provision that allowed landlords to keep land
provided it had been acquired at least forty years before. He
also forbade patronage and vigorously enforced the measures
that compelled men of status to pay the taxes of the poor,
should the latter be unable to do so. There was another side
to this social problem: the monasteries, whose number and
power were considerable, were scarcely less dangerous to the
peasant farmer than to the large landowners. Ordinances of
Romanus Lecapenus in 922 and 924 made it illegal for monasteries to acquire the land of poor citizens; and in 964 Nicephorus Phocas forbade the establishment of new monasteries, and even donations to existing ones.

These measures were ultimately useless. The landed aristocracy and the institution of monasticism were too well entrenched for the emperor to risk acting without their support
or incurring their hostility for any length of time. From the
time of Romanus III, or at least from the beginning of the
reign of Isaac Comnenus, all this was over. The struggle between the large and small landholder, which is the central
drama of the history of Byzantium, had ended in the triumph
of the men of status.

The Schism

We have already seen what is sometimes called the first
schism of Photius, a result of the anathema mutually laid on
each other by pope and patriarch. Basil I, who in the beginning of his reign had replaced Photius by Ignatius, brought

back the former to power on the death of Ignatius. Then, in 879, a council held at Constantinople lifted the anathema that had been laid on Photius. Until quite recently tradition had it that Pope John VIII immediately, in a fit of pique, renewed the anathema on Photius, bringing about a fresh rupture between the churches known as the second schism of Photius. But the work of Francis Dvornik, V. Laurent and V. Grumel has demonstrated that there was no split after the council of 879. On the contrary, Photius was probably given recognition by the pope. For his part, he probably amended certain doctrinal points of his own and underwent reconciliation with the papacy.

Toward the middle of the eleventh century the real and final break between Rome and Byzantium occurred. Relations between them had long been strained, because they were both struggling for influence in southern Italy. But this was insufficient reason to cause a schism. Ultimately, what brought it about was the arrogance and ambition of two men opposed to all concessions: a papal legate, Cardinal Humbert, and a patriarch of Constantinople, Michael Cerularius. The latter, authoritarian and brutal, was unafraid of promoting a personal policy at variance with the one being followed toward the West by Constantine IX. When the papal legates arrived on a mission to Constantinople in 1054, the patriarch refused to make any compromise, and Cardinal Humbert, a man of authority and no mere delegate, then laid on the high altar of Santa Sophia the bull of excommunication against Michael Cerularius and left the city. Cerularius himself called a council at which the papal legates were also excommunicated and the rupture was complete.

It is probable that no one at the time realized its importance. It was not, after all, the first incident of its kind: an edict of excommunication is easy to rescind. But this did not happen, and the schism endured.

The common view is that the schism enfeebled Byzantium politically and prevented it from receiving any assistance from the West when it was troubled by the Turks. Many indications lead us to doubt whether the West would have responded effectively to a call from the East in any case. It can hardly be denied that from a religious point of view the schism proved a triumph for the patriarchate and a serious setback for the papacy, the latter being forced to renounce its pretensions over the Church in the Orient while the patriarchate really lost nothing. Freed from subjection to Rome, the Byzantine patriarchate increased its authority over the other three patriarchates in the East and over the Slavic Christians.

The Civilization

The era of the Macedonians was, in terms of general civilization, one of the most brilliant in the history of Byzantium. We find the first sign of this in the legislative activities of the emperors, who had only misguided contempt for the *Ecloga,* wishing to see it replaced by a compilation more appropriate to the times. Basil I had ambitions in this field, but was only able to complete two preparatory works: a *prochiron* (manual) and an *epanoge* (introduction). Leo VI, however, published a monumental collection of *basilicae,* or imperial laws, in Greek. In fact, this was a synthesis of the legislative work of Justinian, omitting those laws that had fallen into disuse and adding others more recent.

We have a particularly interesting text from the era of

Leo VI: the celebrated *Book of the Prefect* (of Constantinople), only discovered at the end of the last century. Among his other duties, the prefect supervised all the organizations of merchants and tradesmen. It is the list of guilds and the details of their organization that makes this the essential document for knowledge of economic life in Byzantium. In the city we find almost all professions subjected to the strictest control in the interests of the state and the population as a whole.

Everything indicates that there was great economic prosperity in Constantinople; into it poured the merchandise and traders of the world. Indeed, for a long time it played a role comparable to that of Piraeus in the Golden Age of Athens. All this commercial wealth, military glory and rediscovered power was expressed in Byzantine art and literature. There no longer remains the New Church or *Nea* of Basil, built at Constantinople, which was for this age what Santa Sophia was for the Age of Justinian. However, in the provinces we find many monuments that are proof of this renaissance. Indeed, the work, often very Greek in style, especially if we think of the mosaics at Daphni, has led the period to be called the second Golden Age of Byzantine art. In the realm of ideas the era is bounded by the two giant figures of Photius and Psellus, as remarkable for their leaning toward Hellenism as for their intimate knowledge of the classical tradition. At times, undoubtedly, there seems to have been a lack of originality, though this criticism is less true of the artists than of the writers. The century produced encyclopedic works: the *Palatine Anthology*, the *Lexicon* of Suidas, the *Lives of the Saints* of Simeon Metaphrastus. The poetry of John the Geometrician is also worth noting, as well as the epic poems of

Digenis Akritas, the histories of Leo the Deacon and Theophanes, and the entire work of Psellus, a scholar and writer on universal topics. The emperors set the example: Leo VI was called "the Wise" because of his enthusiasm for scholarship and men of learning. Constantine Porphyrogenitus, writer, builder and artist, gave life to the whole intellectual climate of his time. We have his treatises preserved for us: the *Administration of the Empire*, the *Dicourses*, and the *Ceremonies of the Byzantine Court*. Constantine Monomachus did perhaps even more useful work when he created, alongside the Faculty of Philosophy directed by Psellus, a Faculty of Law under John Xiphilinus to train imperial administrators.

The Decline

The death of Theodora in 1056 marks the end of the Macedonian dynasty and the beginning of a new period, characterized by continual antagonism between two factions: the army, recruited regionally and under the control of the powerful local landowners; and the central administration and civil service of the capital.

Constantine Monomachus, with experience of rebellions like those of Maniakes and Tarnikios, launched a policy directed against the army, reducing its total strength and often replacing national troops with mercenaries. From 1056 on the struggle between the two elements was reflected in the succession of emperors, each emperor favoring in turn one or the other. Finally, after the reign of Nicephorus III (Nicephorus Botaniates, 1078-1081), who was *strategus* (governor) of a theme in Asia Minor, the feudal party triumphed conclusively with the accession to power of Alexius Comnenus.

The period was, however, not without troubles that seriously affected the foreign policy of the Macedonians on three fronts. In the West, in 1071, the Normans under Robert Guiscard captured Bari after a siege lasting three years; this meant the fall of the Byzantine Empire in Italy. In the Balkans, the Petchenegs, known as the "Turks of the North," crossed the Danube and, plundering the whole of Macedonia and Thrace, laid siege to Constantinople. The Byzantines had to pay them tribute. In the East, the Seljuk Turks, having made slow progress in Persia and Macedonia, now attacked Byzantine Armenia. In this same fatal year, 1071, Romanus Diogenes was defeated and taken prisoner by the Turkish leader, Alp Arslan, at the battle of Manzikert. It was a brutal revelation of the seriousness of the Turkish danger. Though the frontiers of the empire were still intact all the way from Antioch to Lake Van, the route was a signal for confusion: with the forces of the empire in retreat to the West, the path into Asia Minor was open to the Turks.

7 / BYZANTIUM AND THE CRUSADES; THE DYNASTIES OF THE COMNENI AND THE ANGELI; THE LATIN STATES AND THE GREEK EMPIRE OF NICAEA (1081-1261)

The Dynasty of the Comneni

With Alexius Comnenus the military party and the well-entrenched provincial aristocracy triumphed over the bureaucratic faction of the capital. Alexius himself owed his rise to his military prowess. The Comneni, whose family origins lay probably in Adrianople, had become great landholders in Asia Minor. Alexius reigned from 1081 to 1118, his son, John II, from 1118 to 1143, and the latter's son, Manuel I, from 1143 to 1180. For a century the empire had stability and sound government. Manuel always had his eyes on the West, even taking a French princess, Mary of Antioch, for his second wife. It was she who acted as regent during the reign of the young Alexius II (1180-1183). The latter, however, was deposed in 1183 by a nephew of John II, Andronicus Comnenus, in many ways the most original of the Comneni. He deliberately reversed the course of action of his predecessors: on his accession to power he took a strong action against the Latins, and great numbers of them were massacred in Constantinople. In internal policy he waged a ferocious campaign against the higher echelons of the aristocracy. However, he was deposed in his turn by Isaac Angelus, and his reign only lasted two years.

"Two-thirds of the world's wealth is in Constantinople," declared the Crusaders in amazement. But Byzantium, for political reasons, gradually gave up the source of this prosperity in exchange for the role of mediator between East and West. It was the Italian towns—Pisa, Genoa and in particular Venice—that profited by this.

In religious affairs political interests took precedence over questions of doctrine. In several exchanges with the papacy the emperor seemed ready to recognize the pope's religious authority over the Orient; he had perhaps an illusive hope that this might facilitate the re-establishment of his own authority over the West. And the pope, for his part, in order to deceive the emperor of Germany, with whom he had been in violent conflict for some time, often seemed on the verge of a rapprochement with the Byzantine emperor; reunion had never been more imminent.

But when the empire of the West and the papacy finally settled their differences, there was little likelihood of it happening. The Crusades were to be the final check to such a move. Indeed, attempts at union only encountered the indifference and incomprehension of the Latins and the violent opposition of the Greeks. The latter felt their national pride wounded by the extremes to which Manuel's policy of Latin-loving took him, and by the shocking behavior of the Crusaders.

The Orient and the Balkans

The most serious menace that Alexius I had to face was that of the Petchenegs, a tribe that the Bogomils, members of a heretical Slav nationalist sect owing allegiance to Paulicianism,[1] called in to assist them against Byzantium. The Petchenegs defeated Alexius at Silistria[2] and in 1091 were camped beneath the walls of Constantinople. They were on the point of concluding an extremely dangerous alliance with the Seljuk Turks when Alexius, finding himself cornered, called in the wild Polovtsian tribes against them. In the same year nearly all the Petchenegs were massacred and the Turks, as a result of the First Crusade, were pushed out of Asia Minor for some time. At the beginning of the reign of John II the Petchenegs again attempted to build up an offensive, but they were completely crushed and disappeared from the Byzantine historical scene forever.

John II had other troubles: a further threat arose west of the Balkans from a coalition of two vigorous young nations, the Hungarians and the Serbs. He fought campaigns against both, and these, though indecisive, were sufficient to contain their growing ambitions. However, decisive victories were won by him in Cilicia, where the puppet state of lesser Armenia was established by Armenian refugees, thus bringing about the return of Cilicia into the imperial orbit.

Manuel looked eastward only with reluctance, but he was compelled to take an interest there by an uprising in Cilicia. When he managed to suppress this, the Turkish ques-

[1] A sect with origins in Armenia whose followers believed in the equality of the powers of evil with those of good, assigning to the former the realms of the flesh and to the latter the realms of the spirit.

[2] Also Dorostolon, in Bulgaria.

tion became more important. The sultan of Iconium was, at that time, the formidable Kilij Arslan II, who in 1176 with his Turkish army had cut the Byzantine forces to ribbons at the battle of Myriocephalum. For Byzantium, almost a century after Manzikert, it was the shattering of all hope of defeating the Turks in Asia and a defeat for Manuel's policy in the West. For a vain illusion he had neglected the real and pressing interests of the empire.

The West: Venetians and Normans

Robert Guiscard had already set up the duchy of Apulia in southern Italy, which was to be the beginning of the Kingdom of Sicily; he soon turned his ambitions to the empire also, and seized Dyrrachium (Durazzo), a town on the route across Macedonia and Thrace to Constantinople. Alexius I, having no fleet powerful enough to resist the Normans, sought the protection of the Venetian navy. In return for this he gave the Venetians certain commercial privileges. The result of this agreement was Guiscard's loss of Dyrrachium. However, in order to pay for the services of Venice, Alexius, in 1082, was compelled to grant the Venetians a chrysobull (a document bearing the imperial gold seal), which was one of the most important documents ever signed by the emperor. The practical effect was that Venetian merchants received the right to buy and sell throughout the empire without paying tax or passing through customs control. They also obtained another concession in Constantinople itself, where an area of the city and a number of warehouses were reserved for their use. Indeed, Venetian traders in the empire received more favorable treatment than those of Byzantium herself. This step was of the utmost importance and in taking it Byzantium renounced a portion of those enormous advantages inherent in her position as intermediary between East and West, which had given her economic strength. For Venice, it was the beginning of a tremendous expansion, which gradually brought the Mediterranean world under her influence. Thenceforth she showed herself to be a state that put her maritime strength exclusively to the service of her commercial interests. By an astonishing mixture of cynicism and skill, and the persistence with which she pursued her remarkable policy, she was to realize for several centuries her ambitions of unscrupulous economic imperialism. Indeed, the seed of the Fourth Crusade was sown in the act of 1082.

All that the Byzantine emperors could now do in their efforts to diminish the importance of the privileges granted to the Venetians was to grant comparable privileges to the Venetians' principal rivals, the Pisans and the Genoese. This John II did when he was unable to avoid renewing the chrysobull of 1082. However, when he saw the empire threatened by the ambitions of the young Kingdom of Sicily set up by Roger II, he sought the protection he needed, not from Venice, but from the Emperor of Germany. Nor did his successor, Manuel, abandon the alliance with Conrad III (Manuel's first marriage was to Conrad's sister-in-law). However, when Roger captured Corfu and made a daring raid into Greece (getting as far as Attica), the emperor made a new appeal to Venice. The Venetians obligingly retook Corfu but extracted new economic concessions from Byzantium as payment. Later, when William I succeeded Roger II, Manuel made a second attempt to solve the Norman question with his own forces; but his troops suffered defeat at Brindisi. The Byzantines never again returned to Italy. The Normans, however, invaded the empire a second time, and during the reign of Andronicus recaptured Dyrrachium, also besieging and capturing Thessalonica. After conducting great massacres there they marched toward Constantinople. While this was happening revolution broke out in the capital, and the populace replaced Andronicus with Isaac Angelus, who managed to drive the Normans out of Thessalonica and Dyrrachium. But though the emperors had been able to protect the empire, they had not succeeded in destroying Norman power in Italy. Moreover, this poor achievement had been bought with considerable commercial concessions to the economic imperialism of Venice.

The First Crusades

The Crusades are a complex phenomenon, so often misunderstood because they are only looked at from the Western point of view or in their religious aspect. In fact, the political and economic factors are of prime importance. Religious belief and the deliverance of the holy places were merely the guises that cloaked these interests. Even the popes themselves were not always motivated by pure religious ideals: it was their hope that the schism of 1054 could be resolved in such a way that the Orient would be brought under their spiritual hegemony once more.

The decision to launch the First Crusade was taken by the Council of Clermont at the instigation of Pope Urban II. In the same year an ill-organized band of wretched men was led across Europe by Peter the Hermit and Walter the Penniless. Their numbers are unknown, but everywhere they went they pillaged. Alexius I was greatly disturbed when they presented themselves at the gates of Constantinople and hurried them on their way to Asia Minor, where this lawless, fanatical and half-starved mob was all but wiped out by the Turks near Nicaea. In the following year an army of feudal barons marked their passage through the emperor's lands by further pillaging, again arousing the fears of Alexius. The latter, however, obtained from the Crusaders an oath of allegiance. Nicaea, Edessa and Antioch were all taken by the Crusaders; and finally, on July 15, 1099, Jerusalem itself was captured. The Crusaders set up a number of principalities in the East, on Western feudal models: Baldwin of Flanders became ruler in Edessa, Bohemond of Taranto in Antioch, and Godfrey of Bouillon in Jerusalem. But they forgot that they were considered vassals by the emperor of Byzantium. John II brought this home to them severely when he used his army to re-establish Byzantine sovereignty over Antioch.

The Second Crusade was the result of a new Turkish offensive, which led to the re-capture of Edessa. With the fall of this Frankish principality Jerusalem and Antioch were left dangerously unprotected. The new Crusade was preached by Bernard of Clairvaux and was under the direction of Louis VII of France and the German emperor Conrad III. At this news, Manuel, though particularly fond of the Latins and a relative of Conrad III by marriage, hastily set the fortifications of Constantinople in order. The Germans arrived first, and Manuel spared no effort to help them across into Asia Minor, where they suffered a bloody defeat at the hands of the Turks. A similar reception and fate awaited the army of Louis VII a little later. Eventually, both Conrad III and Louis VII returned to the West. Some years later Manuel inflicted a crushing defeat on Ronald of Chatillon, the Latin prince of Antioch, and made a triumphal entry into his city.

The Third Crusade, a reaction to the campaigns of Saladin, who had set up a new dynasty in Egypt, met with a no

The Greek Orient

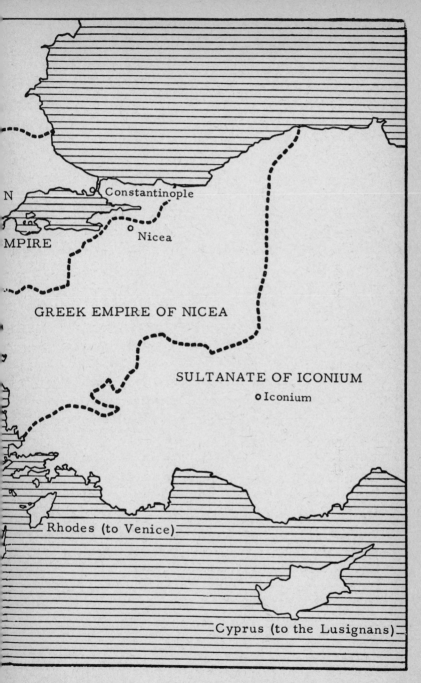

N

MPIRE

Constantinople

Nicea

GREEK EMPIRE OF NICEA

SULTANATE OF ICONIUM

Iconium

Rhodes (to Venice)

Cyprus (to the Lusignans)

after the Crusades

less definite setback. In 1187 Saladin had attacked the kingdom of Jerusalem, taken the city and made the king a prisoner. The leaders of this Crusade were the great rulers of the West: Philip Augustus, Richard the Lion-Hearted and Frederick Barbarossa. The new Crusade filled the emperor, Isaac Angelus, with no less fear than had been felt by his predecessors, Alexius and Manuel, in earlier Crusades. Isaac even sought an understanding with Saladin. However, the army of Barbarossa, which came by land, was defeated in Asia Minor, and the emperor was drowned. Nor did Philip Augustus and Richard, who came by sea, have much success. They failed to retake Jerusalem and returned to the West after some time, disappointed.

From this struggle Islam emeregd victorious. Can the blame for this be put on the duplicity of the empire? Such a view was taken by the West, but it is not a fair judgment. Much more can be attributed to the way the Crusades were prepared and carried out by the Frankish barons. Originally, the Byzantine emperor had only asked the Latins for some mercenaries to help him protect Christianity against the infidels; he never understood the Crusades and was unable to hope for their success, since they would assuredly reduce the East to subservience to the West. He had reason to receive with strong defiance these feudal armies in which the religious zeal of the humble was exploited by the ambitions of their feudal lords. The events of the Fourth Crusade show how well grounded these fears were.

The Fourth Crusade

Its leader was nominally the Italian, Boniface of Montferrat, but the real leaders were Pope Innocent III and Dandolo, the Doge of Venice. Innocent III, an enthusiastic supporter of the unity of the churches (under the direction of Rome, of course), represented the spiritual and religious interests, while Dandolo was the incarnation of the economic ambitions of Venice. It was the latter, however, who played the decisive role, since the Crusaders were to be transported to the East on Venetian ships. The conditions for this were that the price of the transportation should be paid in its entirety before the expedition set out. Since the Crusaders could not immediately collect the necessary sum, Venice obtained the following undertaking from them: they promised to seize the town of Zara, on the eastern shore of the Adriatic, on the doge's behalf to complete payment. (The town had been Venetian but it was then in the possession of the King of Hungary.) It was a strange beginning for a crusade against the infidel, for Zara was a Christian town belonging to a Christian ruler. In spite of the pope's protestations, the Crusaders accepted these extraordinary terms, stormed Zara and gave it back to Venice.

But this was not all. The Crusaders' original objective had been Egypt, on which Palestine depended for its military support. However, in exile in the West was Alexius Angelus, the young son of Isaac Angelus II, who had been deposed by Alexius III. Alexius Angelus was also a relative of the emperor Philip of Swabia. It was the latter who suggested to the Crusaders that they should first re-establish Alexius on the throne, pointing out that it would be to their advantage to have the support of the emperor in the East. Dandolo accepted the idea, realizing the profit Venice might derive from such a situation. What is more surprising is that the Crusaders were converted so easily to this change of destination.

And so the fleet, instead of making for Egypt, set sail for Byzantium, arriving there in June, 1203. What followed is well known. In July of the same year Constantinople was taken by storm, Alexius III was deposed and Isaac Angelus and his son Alexius IV were set in his place. But the Greeks knew full well that these sovereigns were merely soft clay in the hands of the Latins and the pope, and a popular uprising led to their expulsion. In response to this the Crusaders decided to take Constantinople and the empire for themselves. After a siege they finally captured the city, on April 13, 1204. For three days there were the most frightful scenes of bloodshed and looting while the city was sacked; members of the Latin clergy took part in this alongside the soldiers of Christ. Huge quantities of fine treasure dazzled the eyes of the unsophisticated and ignorant Crusaders; what had been gathered here over the centuries in a city hitherto inviolate was scattered through the Western world. It was a fitting conclusion to a crusade that had had so unorthodox a beginning.

The Latin States

The Crusaders now had the task of dividing the plunder and electing a Latin emperor. The choice fell on Baldwin, Count of Flanders, who duly received his crown in Santa Sophia. The Latin patriarch was, however, a Venetian, Thomas Morosin; land in the capital was split between Baldwin and Dandolo, the latter being the only Crusader who owed no allegiance to Baldwin. Venice also acquired Dyrrachium and the Ionian islands, the majority of the Aegean islands, Euboea, Rhodes, Crete and numerous places in the Peloponnesus, the Hellespont and Thrace. The Crusade had given Venice a colonial empire and economic hegemony.

On the wreckage of the Byzantine Empire, alongside the Latin state of Constantinople, a series of Frankish states were set up on the feudal model. These included the kingdom of Thessalonica under Boniface of Montferrat; the duchy of Athens and Thebes under the Frenchman Otto de la Roche; and the principality of Achaea (or Morea), which had been conquered by William of Champlitte and Geoffrey of Ville-hardouin. Of the Greek Empire only three fragments can be considered independent states: the kingdom of Epirus, ruled by the Angeli Comneni; the empire of Trebizond to the southeast of the Black Sea; and the empire of Nicaea.

The Empire of Nicaea

During the time there was a Latin emperor in Constantinople (1204-1261) it was the empire of Nicaea that was the true representative of the Byzantine Empire and the refuge of Hellenism. To Nicaea belongs the credit for finally liberating Byzantium. This state was founded by Theodore Lascaris (1204-1261), who was succeeded by the forceful ruler John III (John Ducas Vatatzes, 1222-1254). From the first it is clear that the Crusaders were not willing to allow this principality to survive. Their armies set out to conquer Asia Minor, which seemed indispensable if they were to maintain their hold on Constantinople. However, they were soon recalled to the West by a great upheaval in the Balkans that brought Greeks and Bulgars together in opposition to the Latins. The campaign was conducted by the Bulgar tsar Kalojean; during it the Crusaders were overwhelmingly defeated at the battle of Adrianople in 1205. (The Second Bulgarian Empire had been founded, at the time of the Angeli dynasty, by Peter and John Asen.) During this battle the Latin emperor Baldwin disappeared, either killed or taken prisoner. Soon after this Dandolo also died. Indeed, from its very beginnings Frankish domination in the Orient had been crumbling. The battle also meant that the empire of Nicaea was safe, a situation further confirmed by the brilliant victory of Theodore Lascaris over the sultan of Iconium. Thenceforth it became certain that the Byzantine Empire would again be formed and that this would be at Nicaea's instigation. But fifty confused years intervened, and in the meantime the Latin Empire centered on Constantinople lived on, a heavy burden even to itself.

Baldwin's successor in Constantinople, his brother Henry, was victorious in his early battles and made deep inroads into Asia Minor, until John Vatatzes turned the tide by defeating the Latins, crossing into Europe where he seized Adrianople and began a march on Constantinople. It is certain that he encountered the hostility of the rulers of Epirus, who on destroying the Latin kingdom of Thessalonica were counting on recapturing Constantinople for themselves. But Theodore Angelus, their ruler, was defeated at Clotonica, between Adrianople and Philoppopolis, and taken prisoner by the forces of the Bulgar tsar, John Asen II. In 1241 Asen died and John Vatatzes took the opportunity to return to Europe, retaking from the Bulgars their conquests in Macedonia and Thrace. He also captured Thessalonica and brought Epirus under his authority.

His work was completed, not by his successor Theodore II (Theodore Lascaris), who died in 1258, nor by the latter's son, John IV (1258-1261), who was only seven years old when he came to the throne, but by Michael Palaeologus, a relative of John Vatatzes who, profiting by John IV's minority, began to play an important role. First, in 1259, he defeated the ruler of Epirus and his ally William of Villehardouin, Prince of Achaea, at Pelagonia in western Macedonia, taking Villehardouin prisoner; then, on July 25, 1261, his forces succeeded in capturing Constantinople without great loss. The Latin emperor, Baldwin II, and his Latin patriarch, fled to the West. The empire of the Latins had collapsed; for some years previously it had been eking out a miserable and precarious existence, the emperor making money to support himself by selling relics, and burning timber from the framework of his palace to keep warm. The reconstructed Byzantine Empire was in a similar condition; after the crises it had been through it was in the state of exhaustion that, after two centuries of decline, led to its final collapse.

8 / THE PALAEOLOGI AND THE FALL OF THE BYZANTINE EMPIRE (1261-1453)

General Characteristics

When the Crusades and the Latin domination left the Greek Orient in 1261, the empire was only a shadow of what it had been under the Comneni; it was economically exhausted and territorially fragmented. In Constantinople palaces and entire districts had fallen into ruins; indeed, the city had not recovered from the terrible sacking of 1204. The provinces presented the same image as the capital. It seemed utopian to hope for a return to prosperity when the sources of prosperity had passed from Greek hands. Now the merchant republics of Venice and Genoa were exploiting the market of the Greek Orient for their own profit. This was indeed the most important and lasting result of the Crusades. In Asia the empire was left with the territory of the Nicaean Empire; in Europe, with Thrace and a part of Macedonia. Charles Diehl calls it a "sick, weak and wretched body with an enormous head, Constantinople." All around were states either independent or hostile: the empire of Trebizond, which continued to exist until the Turkish conquest; the kingdom of Epirus and the duchy of Neopatras, Greek states that had little desire to accept Byzantine authority; the duchy of Athens, which passed from the hands of the French into those of the Catalans, and the principality of Morea, which took more than a century to get back into the bosom of the empire; and finally almost all the Aegean islands and a large number of coastal places that had been divided between the Genoans and the Venetians. Further away still and witnessing the agony of this dismembered empire, called "the sick man of the Middle Ages," were the Turks, the states of the West, and Serbia and Bulgaria.

Such was the situation when the forces of Michael VIII surprised the defenseless Constantinople. In the last stage of the history of Constantinople (1261-1453) two periods can be distinguished, very unequal in length. In the first period we have the reign of Michael; in the second, that of his successors. The year 1282, the date of the death of Michael and the succession of Andronicus II, marks in effect a complete break. The reign of Michael VIII, restorer and continuer of Byzantium, can definitely be treated as a stage in the empire of Nicaea; the history of the Palaeologi and of Byzantine decadence begins with Andronicus II. Michael VIII had the task of finishing off the struggle with the Latins and preventing Western retaliation against the East. His energy and the success of his policy made his the last great reign in the history of Byzantium. But it was not in his power to cure the deep-seated malaise of an empire in decay, exhausted internally and threatened externally, and his successors could only confine themselves to postponing the evil day. Andronicus II

(1282-1328) and Andronicus III (1328-1341) saw the Turks become masters of Asia Minor. John V (1341-1392) and the usurper John VI (1341-1355) saw the Serbs of Stephen Dushan at the gates of Constantinople, and the first Turkish conquests in Europe. Under Manuel II (1391-1425) and John VIII (1425-1448) the progress of the Turks reduced the empire to its capital and suburbs. The humiliating voyages that these two emperors made to the West to beg assistance were unfruitful. As Diehl says: "The only consideration of the West was how to profit from the misfortunes of the Greek Empire, to dominate her in religion, conquer her politically and exploit her economically." The inevitable collapse came on May 29, 1453, when the last Byzantine emperor, Constantine XI, died heroically on the battlements of Constantinople as they were stormed by the Turks.

The internal history of the empire during this long period is little known. The emperors had to surmount enormous financial difficulties; they worked especially hard at subjecting to taxation property previously exempt. The result was not always satisfactory. Michael VIII, in imposing taxes on soldiers serving on the Eastern frontier (who had previously been exempt from dues and taxes), perhaps upset them dangerously. Moreover, it should be stressed that these measures could scarcely be effective in a situation in which all trade was in the hands of foreigners. A chronicler relates how at the wedding of John V there was not a gold or silver goblet in the palace, and the garments worn were not embroidered as of old with precious stones but merely with chips of colored glass. The empire no longer had the money to maintain a fleet; the mercenaries in the army were poorly paid and always ready for revolt, disloyalty or plunder.

As ever in Byzantium, religious conflict provided a mirror image of the political disturbances; this was especially so in the continuous squabbling over the union with Rome. The activity of the Zealots (sometimes called Arseniates, after the patriarch Arsen) brought back memories of the Studites. Like them, the Zealots relied on the monks and the populace to defend a pure form of orthodoxy and oppose the emperor's policy, if necessary by treason. This was another victory for the monks and Oriental mysticism and a defeat for moderates and rationalists prepared to accept a compromise with Rome. It represented a triumph for the contemplative doctrine of Hesychasm (derived from a Greek word meaning tranquillity or calm). Its ardent defender against Barlaam of Calabria was Gregory Palamas, a monk from Mount Athos who became Archbishop of Thessalonica, one of the most curious figures in the history of Byzantium.

The epoch of the Palaeologi was, moreover, one of great prosperity for monasteries on the lines of Mount Athos; they gave Constantinople a long series of patriarchs. For the most civilized men in Byzantium the monasteries represented a place of retreat and meditation in the midst of these distressed times. Many went into them and ended their lives wearing a monk's habit.

The last two centuries of the empire, in many ways so disappointing, were not, however, times of intellectual poverty. On the contrary, literature and the arts shone with such brilliance that the period has been called "the second Byzantine renaissance." Comparison has often been made with the Italian renaissance. Its most remarkable feature was a return to the traditions and study of the spirit behind the ancient Greek civilization, very marked in the case of the writers but also found among artists. At Constantinople the mosaics of the church of Chora (Kahrich Djami) are the masterpiece of the period. During this era Byzantine civilization had a profound influence on Serbia, Russia and Rumania. Within the empire two great artistic schools opposed one another: the so-called Macedonian school, which includes among its achievements the decoration of most of the ancient churches of Mount Athos; and the incorrectly titled Cretan school, whose most beautiful work can still be seen today in the churches of Mistra.

The name Mistra recalls what was perhaps the most unique characteristic of this period. For at this time intellectual and even political life gradually began to withdraw from Constantinople, which was too exposed to danger, and to take refuge in the Peloponnesus. Here life was not only more secure, but was also nearer the ancient and glorious traditions of Greek civilization; on these Byzantium, itself near to death, began to look with affection, seeking both an example and a consolation. From the beginning of the reign of Michael VIII the reconquest of the Frankish principality of Achaea had moved apace: three places, Monemvasia, Moina and Mistra, were in effect the ransom paid in 1262 for William of Villehardouin, who had been imprisoned at Pelagonia by the Byzantines. Then Michael VIII recaptured Arcadia and Laconia and his successors managed to make Morea once more a Greek territory. Mistra, near the site of ancient Sparta, where the Villehardouins had built a powerful castle, was the most important town. From the time of John VI, the title "Ruler of Mistra" was in the prerogative of the second son of the emperor reigning in Byzantium. Yet it was less a province of the empire than a real independent state. The hill of Mistra was covered with villas, churches and monasteries, and the Ruler's court was even more brilliant and lively than that of Constantinople. Here lived eminent scholars, among them the celebrated philosopher and humanist Gemistus Pletho, who presented Manuel II with schemes for reform designed to regenerate Greece. Indeed, at the point when Hellenism was on the verge of being plunged into darkness for several centuries, it was on the very soil of ancient Greece that it threw forth its last rays.

Michael VIII Palaeologus

It was toward the West that Michael VIII, the refounder of the empire, turned his attention. Byzantium had three enemies there: Venice and the papacy, both desiring, one for economic and the other for religious reasons, the restoration of the Latin Empire; and the new sovereign of the Kingdom of the Two Sicilies, Charles of Anjou, a brother of Saint Louis. The latter made much of political rights: by a treaty signed at Viterbo he forced the exiled emperor Baldwin II to cede him his rights over the Latin Empire. Charles is suspected of having made himself the instrument of Venetian and papal designs. Such a formidable coalition might indeed have prevented the Greek Empire, hardly yet re-formed, from surviving, and Michael VIII's reign was devoted to averting this danger. At times the emperor had recourse to arms, achieving success against the Angevin forces in Epirus, the Venetians in Euboea, and the Franks in Morea. But the exhaustion of the empire did not permit a policy of military expansion, and Michael prefered to use Byzantium's favorite weapon—diplomacy.

Venice. To combat the Venetians Michael came to an understanding with Genoa; in March, 1621, at Nymphaeum a treaty was signed that granted the Genoese considerable commercial rights over all the present and future territories of the empire, in exchange for which the Genoese fleet was to give the emperor assistance. There were, of course, several misunderstandings: when, for example, the Genoese seemed to be supporting the ambitious projects of King Manfred of Sicily, who wanted to recapture Constantinople from the Greeks, Michael VIII responded by driving the Genoese from the capital. This incident, however, was quite minor, and Michael soon gave the Genoese back all their privileges. Under the Palaeologi the Genoese took the place in the Orient so long occupied by the Venetians. In 1453 it was a Genoese, Giustiniani, who took charge of the defense of Constantinople against the Turks.

The Papacy. Michael VIII's policy was one of concession to the pope: in 1274 at Lyons he concluded an agreement that placed the Eastern church under the authority of the pope. It was indeed the sole policy that could prevent the papacy from supporting and directing the formidable strength of Charles of Anjou against Byzantium. It is in this guise that the religious policy of Michael VIII should be judged. But the Greeks were unwilling to see the acceptance of unqualified Roman claims, and violent opposition, directed, of course, by the monks, flared up against the emperor, who was stigmatized by the epithet "Latin-minded" (*Latinophrone*). The matter almost turned into a schism within the Greek Church, when Michael, with the help of the patriarch John Bekkos, wanted to impose the Latin union by force. But the agreement of Lyons was in the end to become a dead letter, though it had nonetheless played a useful role in the policy of Michael VIII.

Charles of Anjou. Charles was in fact the most dangerous adversary of all. For a long time Michael VIII used force and diplomacy in turn against him; this continued until the decisive event of the Sicilian Vespers. On March 31, 1282, a violent rebellion against Angevin rule broke out at Palermo and spread throughout Sicily. Everywhere Frenchmen were massacred. The causes of the uprising were numerous; the harshness of French administration and the Sicilian ambitions of Peter of Aragon played their part. However, it is certain that the intrigues of Michael, as well as the subsidies he paid to Peter of Aragon, were also very important. The Byzantine emperor's calculations were accurate: Charles of Anjou, who was at that time in the Orient leading an expedition against the Greek Empire, was forced to return hastily to the West; but he lost Sicily after all. For Byzantium, the Western danger vanished and Michael VIII had completed his task. In the same year, 1282, he died.

The Early Successors of Michael VIII

Michael's reign, when considered as a whole, had been both fortunate and brilliant. Yet preventing the West from again setting foot in the empire can only be considered a negative result. Perhaps it had even prevented him from turning his attention sufficiently toward the East. On this front his successors now had to face the double threat from the Serbs and the Turks.

The Serbs. The first Serbian state had been founded in the seventh century by Stephen Nemanya. His successors, by a series of conquests over the Bulgars and the Greeks, had made Serbia the most powerful state in the Balkans, reaching its heyday under Stephen Dushan, who came to the throne in 1331. Like all rulers who gained power in the Balkans, Du-

shan had the dream of capturing Constantinople. According-
ly, at the beginning of the reign of Andronicus III, he marched
into northern Macedonia and Albania. Profiting by the youth
of John V and the serious disorder caused by the rivalry between John and John VI, Dushan seized all of Macedonia
except Thessalonica. Capturing Serres, he was proclaimed
"Emperor of the Serbs and Romans" (i.e., the Greeks), and
crowned himself with an imperial crown in 1346 at Skoplje.
All he had to do was to capture Constantinople; but it seemed
that the Serbian ruler failed in his efforts to achieve an alliance either with Venice (for he needed a fleet) or with the
Turks. It is likely that he never undertook the great expedition that chroniclers place in 1355. In the same year Dushan
died; the power of his empire did not survive him and Byzantium was saved.

The Turks. A Turkish tribe, forced westward by the
Mongols in the movement that carried the latter into Asia
Minor, had been organized into a powerful state by their
leader, Osman, who founded the dynasty of the Ottomans.
Very suddenly the expansionist movement of the Ottomans
seemed threatening to Byzantium. She had to accept the assistance offered by a company of Catalan mercenaries once
in the pay of Peter of Aragon, but now unemployed. These
mercenaries were at first victorious over the Turks, but they
soon fell out with Byzantium and turned against her. Install-
ing themselves in Gallipoli, they threatened the capital for
three years. Then, after laying waste Thrace and Macedonia,
and being checked only before the walls of Thessalonica, they
went on to invade Thessaly and the duchy of Athens, where
they were easily successful against the heavily armored
Frankish knights at the battle of Lake Copais in 1311. Here

they now set up the Catalan duchy of Athens. This extraordinary adventure of a wandering army no more than several thousand soldiers strong revealed well enough the weakness of the empire.

The Turks, however, kept up their progress, taking Brusa in 1329 (and making it their capital), Nicaea in 1329, and Nicomedia in 1337. By 1341, at the death of Andronicus III, they were practically masters of Asia Minor, and already beginning to make raids into Thrace. Like the Serbs, they took advantage of the internal squabbling in Byzantium under John V. John VI, who had married his daughter to Sultan Orhan, and who was relying on the Turks to help him to the throne, called them into Thrace, ceding them a fortified place on the European bank of the Straits. From then on the Turks never ceased to intervene directly in the affairs of the empire. They installed themselves in fortifications in the region of Gallipoli, which was their base for their march into the Balkans. Murad I conquered Thrace, Philippopolis and Adrianople, making the latter his capital in 1365. It was a certain sign of the European ambitions of the Turks. In the face of this threatening danger, John V sought a rapprochement with the West, and journeying to Rome in 1369, made a confession of faith in conformity with Catholic dogma, recognizing the pope as the head of the Christian Church. This agreement was to be as futile as that made at Lyons. On his way back through Venice, the unfortunate Emperor of Byzantium was arrested by the Venetians for bankruptcy and his son Manuel had to hastily collect the sum demanded. Meanwhile the Turks were continuing to advance. In 1389 they crushed the Serbian imperial might at the great battle of Kossovo; and after Serbia, Bulgaria soon passed under their control.

The Last Palaeologi

These events made the Turks neighbors of Hungary, and the Hungarian ruler, Sigismund, sought aid from the West; a feeble contingent was sent, only to be annihilated at the battle of Nicopolis in 1396. The successor of John V, Manuel II, likewise appealed for help. Charles VI of France sent him Marshal Boucicaut and 1,200 men. But although the marshal got the better of the Turks in a large number of engagements on the outskirts of Constantinople, he did not have sufficient forces to undertake a real campaign. In 1399 Manuel II and Boucicaut left for the West to seek subsidies and troops. Manuel undertook a kind of pilgrimage, traveling to Venice and other Italian cities and to Paris where he was lodged in magnificence at the Louvre by Charles VI. He also went to London, where he obtained many promises, which came to nothing. Back in Paris again he stayed a further two years without success. It was here that, in 1402, he learned of the bloody defeat inflicted on Sultan Bajazet at Ankara by the savage Moguls under Tamerlane. For some time the attention and efforts of the Turks were to be deflected from Byzantium, and Manuel hastened to return and enjoy his few years of respite. But again, in 1422, a mere twenty years after the defeat at Ankara, Sultan Murad II brought a Turkish army in sight of Constantinople.

In 1430, in the reign of John VIII, the Turks besieged Thessalonica, which the Greeks, in order to save it from the infidel, had at the last moment given to Venice. Nonetheless the town was taken by storm. John VIII in his turn left for the West, and like his predecessors, agreed to recognize papal supremacy in the hope of obtaining effective help from the Latins. At the Council of Florence (1439) John VIII (assisted by the famous Cardinal Bessarion) and Pope Eugene IV proclaimed the Decree of Union, which satisfied all Catholic and Roman demands. As at Lyons and Rome, the concessions were to no avail. In the East they were resisted by the majority of the population and the Byzantine clergy; and in the West no serious effort was made to defend Christianity from the Turks. The pope did succeed in mustering a small army of Hungarians, Poles and Rumanians, under the command of Vladislav II, King of Hungary, but it was wiped out at the battle of Varna in 1444. No other attempt was made.

Byzantium was abandoned to its fate and events moved fast. In 1451 Mohammed II became sultan, and on the European bank of the Bosphorus, quite close to Constantinople, built a fortress, Roumeli Hissar, that cut the lines of communication between Byzantium and the Black Sea. Then, after leading an expedition against Morea to prevent any assistance coming from that quarter, he took up his position in front of Constantinople in April, 1453. The city was valiantly defended by the emperor Constantine Dragases, by the inhabitants, and by Giustiniani the Genoese. But the Turks, who had a considerable army at their disposal and a powerful corps of siege artillery, succeeded in forcing breaches in the ancient Theodosian walls. By a clever piece of strategy they were able to break the Byzantine defense, and during one night they brought their fleet from the Sea of Marmara into the Golden Horn; Greek resistance was growing weaker, and the final assault was fixed for dawn on May 29. This fact became known in the beleaguered city. On the day before, processions filed through the streets; in the evening the last Christian office was celebrated at Santa Sophia, and the emperor, with a great number of people, received the last sacraments.

The next day he was to fall heroically on the battlements. When Mohammed II rode into Santa Sophia on horseback, he found the vast nave carpeted with people who had sought refuge there and had been slaughtered. Three days and three nights were given over to pillage, massacre and brutality of every kind.

Finally, in 1460, Mohammed II came in person to capture Mistra. In the following year, after he had taken Trebizond, nothing remained of the Greek Empire.

CONCLUSION

The fall of Byzantium was doubtless due to the obsolescence of its institutions of government and the internal faults of a state built upon authoritarian principles without the elasticity to reform itself. But there were two other causes of particular importance, which are, in fact, linked: the Crusades and the religious conflict between East and West.

The Crusades ruined Byzantium—a ruin that was completely pointless, since the Franks were incapable of maintaining their states in the Orient and of achieving lasting political works. Byzantium never recovered from the blows she had sustained. The era of the Palaeologi, one long agony, was built from what could be salvaged from the wreck. True, it had some fine new bursts of vitality, but there was no resurrection. Byzantium was worn out; the economic tyranny of the merchants of Venice and Genoa forbade its recovery. Indeed the financial conquest of the empire by the West had been completed long before the Turks made their territorial gains.

The sole hope of salvation had lain in an understanding between Greeks and Latins for the defense of Christianity. Of all the reasons that made such an entente impossible the most important was, in fact, that of religion. All the efforts (credit should also be given to the spirit of tolerance shown by the Palaeologi) foundered against the pretensions of the papacy, the incomprehension and greed of the Latins, and the obstinacy of the Greeks. Two examples will serve to show how deep-seated this disagreement was. Petrarch had the audacity to write: "The Turks are our enemies, but the schismatic Greeks are worse than enemies." And at the same time a great dignitary of Byzantium declared: "It would be better to see the turban of the Turks reigning in Constantinople than the miter of the Latins." Such were the reasons why Byzantium alone had to bear the full force of the Turks.

However, with Byzantium in the hands of the Turks, the disappearance of the Greek Empire left a large vacuum in the world. For eleven centuries it had played a role, always important and often decisive, in the history of East and West. From the wavering hands of Rome Byzantium had received the heritage of the ancient world at the moment when it was about to disappear under the flood-tide of the barbarian invasion. Before succumbing in its turn to buffets from new invaders, it had managed to play its part in preserving, enriching and passing on this heritage.

Byzantium preserved this heritage through the long, inconclusive and troubled period we call the Middle Ages. It defended it against the attacks of innumerable peoples. It is indeed a moving spectacle to witness this empire—so often assailed, its capital facing siege on so many occasions—arraigned against all the peoples of north, south, east and west, yet succeeding in thwarting their attacks.

Byzantium enriched the heritage, too, by bringing in Christianity and contact with the Orient. From a pagan civilization in the grip of decadence and incapable of self-renewal, Byzantium created a Christian one, more humane and responsive to the dictates of a critical conscience. And while assuring to ancient Hellenism this continuity of tradition—and the continuity of the Greek language was both a symbol and Byzantium's finest instrument—it added to it, both in art and in thought, the fruits of a long intercourse with the Persian and Moslem Orient.

Finally, Byzantium transmitted this heritage through its scholars, missionaries, traders and soldiers to all the peoples with whom it came in contact. In the East Byzantium was not limited to mere borrowing: the Arabs and Turks themselves came deeply under its influence. The Slavs owe the whole of their religion and their institutions to it. Western countries, through merchants, monks, pilgrims and Crusaders, never ceased to be under the magic of far-off and beguiling Constantinople. It was indeed to the West that Byzantium transmitted its final message, when, after the conquest of the Turks, crowds of learned Greeks came bringing their knowledge and the remnants of their libraries.

BIBLIOGRAPHY

Baynes, Norman H. *The Byzantine Empire.* New York: Oxford University Press.
———, and H. St. L. B. Moss (eds.). *Byzantium: An Introduction to East Roman Civilization.* New York: Oxford University Press, 1948. (Paperback.)
Dalton, O. M. *East Christian Art: A Survey of the Monuments.* Oxford: Oxford University Press, 1925.
Diehl, Charles. *Byzantium: Greatness and Decline.* New Brunswick, N.J.: Rutgers University Press, 1956.
Hussey, J. M. *The Byzantine World.* New York: Hillary House Publishers.
Ostrogorsky, George. *History of the Byzantine State.* New Brunswick, N.J.: Rutgers University Press, 1957.
Rice, David T. *The Byzantines.* London, 1962.
Runciman, Steven. *Byzantine Civilization.* New York: Meridian Books. (Paperback.)
Vasiliev, Alexander A. *History of the Byzantine Empire.* 2 vols. Madison, Wis.: University of Wisconsin Press, 1952. (Paperback.)
Zernov, Nicholas. *Eastern Christendom.* (Putnam's History of Religion, Vol. II.) New York: G. P. Putnam's Sons, 1961.

INDEX

Abyssinia, 32, 61
Achaea, 115, 123
Acroinon, battle of, 79
Adrianople, 8, 13, 40, 94, 103,
    116, 128
    battle of (1205), 115-16
Africa, 49, 63
Agapetus, Pope, 58
Akritas, Digenis, 101
Alaric, 40-41
Albertini, E., 24
Alexander (son of Basil I), 88
Alexandria, 20, 35, 36, 39, 67,
    70, 73
Alexius II, 103
Alexius III, 113, 114
Alexius IV, 114
Amalasontha, 48
Ambrose, Bishop, 31, 35
Amorian dynasty, 78, 81, 88
Anastasius, 30, 42, 45, 50, 58
Anatolia, 77, 78
Anchialus, battle of, 80
Andronicus, 108
Andronicus II, 120
Andronicus III, 121, 127, 128
Angelus, Alexius, 113
Angelus, Isaac, 104, 108, 112
Angelus, Isaac II, 113, 114
Angelus, Theodore, 116
Anthemius of Tralles, 62

Anthimius, Bishop, 58
Antioch, 20, 35, 36, 39, 49, 67,
    73, 90, 109
Antonine dynasty, 4
Arabs, 66, 67, 69-71, 72, 78,
    79-80, 84, 89-91, 94, 135
Arcadius, 29-30, 36, 40, 41
Arcasius, 39
Arianism, 15, 16, 33, 34, 36, 58
Arius, 15, 16, 36
Armenia, 32, 67, 72, 90, 102,
    105
Arseniates, 122
Arslan, Alp, 102
Arslan II, 106
Asen, John, 115
Asen, John II, 116
Asen, Peter, 115
Aspar, Alain, 40
Athanasius of Alexandria, 16, 36
Athens, 115, 120, 127, 128
    University of, 58
Attila, 40, 41-42
Augustus, 3, 4, 21, 27
Aurelian, 4, 5, 23
Avars, 63, 67

Bagratids, 90
Bajazet, Sultan, 129
Baldwin of Flanders, 109, 114,
    116

Baldwin II, 117, 124
Bardas, 78, 80, 85, 88
Bari, 80, 90, 102
Barlaam of Calabria, 122
Basil I, 88, 89, 97, 99
Basil II, 89, 90, 91, 95-97
Bekkos, John, 125
Belisarius, 48, 49, 54
Berbers, 48
Bernard of Clairvaux, 109
Bessarion, Cardinal, 130
Bohemond of Taranto, 109
Boniface of Montferrat, 112, 115
Boris, 80, 85, 91
Boucicaut, Marshal, 129
Bréhier, Louis, 20
Brindisi, 107
Bulgaria, 68-69, 91, 94-95, 120, 128
Bulgars, 69, 72, 78, 79, 80-81, 85, 95, 115, 116, 126

Caesaropapism, 35
Carthage, 63, 71, 72
Catalaunia, 41
Celestine, Bishop, 37
Cerularius, Michael, 98
Chalcedon, Council of, 32, 38, 39, 59
Charles of Anjou, 124, 125-26
Charles VI, 129
Chosroes, 48, 49
Chosroes II, 67
Christianity, 3, 4, 8-17, 29, 31-39, 49, 52, 55, 58-59, 80, 83, 85, 112, 130, 134, 135
Chrysostonius, John, 36
Cilicia, 90, 105
Clermont, Council of, 108
Clovis, 42
Code of Justinian, 53
Comnenus, Alexius, 101, 103, 105, 106, 108, 109, 112
Comnenus, Andronicus, 103-4
Comnenus, Isaac, 97
Conrad III, 107, 109
Constant II, 65, 68

Constantia, 16
Constantine, 3-27, 29, 34, 62
Constantine IV, 65, 69, 70, 71, 74
Constantine V, 77, 79, 80, 81, 82, 85
Constantine VI, 77
Constantine VII, 88-89, 101
Constantine VIII, 89
Constantine IX, 98
Constantine XI, 121
Constantine Monomachus, 89, 90, 101
Constantine the Younger, 8, 29
Constantinople: captured by Crusaders, 114
    Council of, 36, 58, 74, 82, 98
    founding of, 17-21, 31
Constantius, 8, 32, 33, 34
Constantius Chlorus, 6, 7, 29
Corpus Juris Civilis, 52
Crete, 80, 90, 114
Crispus, 8
Crusades, 67, 104, 105, 107, 108-114, 119, 133
Cyprus, 70, 90
Cyrenaica, 70
Cyril, Bishop, 37, 38

Damascus, 70, 90
Dandolo, 112-13, 114, 116
Decree of Union, 130
Demetrius, 68
Diehl, Charles, 47, 65, 119, 121
Diocletian, 5-6, 8, 21, 22, 23, 25
Diogenes, Romanus, 102
Dioscorus, 37, 38
Donatism, 14
Dragases, Constantine, 130
Dushan, Stephen, 121, 126-27
Dvornik, Francis, 98
Dyrrachium, 106, 108, 114

Ecloga, 78, 99
Edessa, 90, 109
Egypt, 36, 37, 38, 39, 58, 60, 70, 71, 73, 109, 113, 114
Ephesus: Council of (431), 37

Council of (449), 38
Epirus, 68, 115, 116, 117, 120, 124
Euboea, 114, 124
Eugene IV, Pope, 130
Eusebius of Caesarea, 9, 10, 11, 12, 13, 18
Eusebius of Nicodemia, 16
Eutyches, 37

Fallmerayer, Jakob, 63
Florence, Council of, 129
Franks, 42, 124, 133
Frederick Barbarossa, 112
Frumentius, 32

Gainus, 40
Galerius, 6, 7, 10-11
Gallipoli, 127, 128
Gaul, 22, 33, 41, 42, 49
Genoa, 104, 119, 124, 133
Geoffrey of Villehardouin, 115
Giustiniani, 125, 130
Godfrey of Bouillon, 109
Goths, 18, 19, 32, 36, 40
Gratianus, 34
Greece, 50, 62, 72, 73, 107, 124
    settlement of Slavs in, 67-68
Gregoire, H., 9, 11
Gregory the Great, Pope, 63-64
Gregory the Illuminator, 32
Grumel, V., 98
Guiscard, Robert, 102, 106

Hadrian, 4, 5, 21, 23, 24, 53
Heraclius, 64, 65-67, 70, 73, 77
Heretics, 29, 34, 35, 36-39, 58
Hesychasm, 122
Honorius, 29, 30, 41
Humbert, Cardinal, 98
Hungarians, 91, 95, 105, 130
Huns, 40, 41-42, 47, 50

Iconium, 106, 116
Iconoclasm, 78, 81-86
Ignatius, Patriarch, 86, 97-98
Igor, Prince, 95
Illyricum, 41, 68

Innocent III, Pope, 112, 113
Irene, Empress, 77-78, 79, 80, 82
Isaurian dynasty, 77
Isidore of Miletus, 62
Islam, 69, 91, 112
Italy, 4, 5, 18, 19, 21, 22, 42, 47, 48, 49, 63, 85, 90, 91, 98, 102, 104, 106, 107, 108

Jerusalem, 67, 70, 90, 109, 112
John II, 103, 105, 107, 109
John III, 115, 116
John IV, 116
John V, 121, 127, 128, 129
John V, 121, 123, 127, 128
John VIII, 121, 129
John of Cappadocia, 54
John the Ascetic, 64
John the Geometrician, 100
Julian, 29, 33, 47
Justin, 45, 55
Justin II, 63
Justinian, 3, 29, 43, 45-64, 66, 70, 71, 74, 79, 85, 87, 99, 100
Justinian II, 65, 68

Kossovo, battle of, 128
Krum, Khan, 80

Lactantius, 10, 11, 12
Lascaris, Theodore, 115, 116
Laurent, V., 98
Lecapenus, Romanus, 88, 89, 90, 94, 95, 96-97
Leo I, 30, 40, 42
Leo III, 77, 79, 80, 81, 82
Leo IV, 77
Leo V, 78, 80, 81
Leo VI, 88, 89, 90, 91, 94, 99, 100, 101
Leo the Deacon, 101
Leo the Great, Pope, 31-32, 37, 38
Licinius, 7, 8, 11, 12, 13, 19
Licinius the Younger, 8
Lombards, 63, 72, 85

Lot, Ferdinand, 25
Louis II, 91
Louis VII, 109
Louis the Pious, 80

Macedonia, 68, 80, 88, 94, 102,
    116, 117, 119, 127
Macedonian dynasty, 79, 87-102
Malamir, 80
Manfred, King, 125
Maniakes, George, 91, 101
Manuel I, 103, 104, 105, 106,
    107, 109, 112
Manuel II, 121, 124, 129
Manzikert, battle of, 102, 106
Marcianus, 30, 38, 40, 41
Martel, Charles, 79
Mary of Antioch, 103
Maxentius, 7, 8, 9, 11, 13
Maximian, 6, 7
Maximinus, 7, 8, 11, 12
Mesopotamia, 70, 80, 90
Metaphrastus, Simeon, 100
Methodius, 85
Michael II, 78, 79, 82
Michael III, 78, 81, 88
Michael IV, 91
Michael VIII, 120, 121, 123,
    124-26
Milan, 19
    Edict of, 11
Milvian bridge, battle of the, 8,
    9, 11
Mistra, 123-24, 131
Moesia, 40, 41, 68
Moguls, 129
Mohammed II, 130-31
Mongols, 127
Monasticism, 60, 84, 97, 122
Monemvasia, 123
Monophysitism, 37-39, 47, 58,
    59, 66, 70, 74
Monotheism, 4
Monothelitism, 70, 74
Moors, 72
Moravia, 85
Morea, 115, 120, 123, 124, 130
Morosin, Thomas, 114

Murad I, 128
Murad II, 129
Myriocephalum, battle of, 106

Naïssus, 41
Nemanya, Stephen, 126
Neopatras, 120
Nestorians, 32
Nestorius, 36-37
Nicaea, 109, 128
    Council of (787), 82, 83
    Empire of, 115-17, 119, 120
Nicaean Creed, 15, 34, 36, 38
Nicephorus I, 78, 80, 82, 84
Nicephorus III, 101
Nicholas I, Pope, 86
Nicomedia, 19, 128
Nika insurrection, 46, 53, 62
Nineveh, 67
Normans, 102, 106, 107-8
North Africa, 43, 47-48, 71, 80
Nymphaeum, 124

Octavius Caesar, 6n.
Odoacer, 30, 42
Oleg, Prince, 95
Omortag, 80
Opsikion, theme of, 72
Orhan, Sultan, 128
Osman, 127
Ostrogorsky, George, 65
Ostrogoths, 40, 42, 47, 48
Otto, 91
Otto II, 91

Paganism, 3, 4, 8, 10, 11, 13,
    14, 17, 18, 58, 83, 135
    end of, 32-34
Palaeologi, 120, 122, 125, 133,
    134
Palaeologus, Michael, 116-17
Palamas, Gregory, 122
Palestine, 60, 70, 71, 90, 113
Paulician sect, 84, 105
Pelagonia, 117, 123
Pepin the Short, 85
Persia, 32, 61, 71, 102
    decline of, 66-67

Persians, 18, 33, 39, 41, 48, 49, 61, 64, 66-67, 70, 73
Petchenegs, 91, 95, 102, 105
Peter of Aragon, 126, 127
Peter the Hermit, 108
Petrarch, 134
Philip Augustus, 112
Philip of Swabia, 113
Philippopolis, 128
Phocas, 63, 64
Phocas, Bardas, 96
Phocas, Nicephorus, 88, 90, 91, 94, 97
Photius, 81, 86, 97-98, 100
Pisa, 104
Plato, Abbot, 84
Pletho, Gemistus, 124
Poitiers, 79
Poles, 130
Procopius, 51, 52
Psellus, 100, 101
Pulcheria, 30

Ravenna, 42, 48, 61, 63, 72, 85
Reggio, 89
Religion, 3, 4, 8-17, 31-39, 55, 58-59, 63, 66, 69-70, 78, 80, 81-86, 104, 108, 121, 122, 124, 133, 134, 135
Rhodes, 70, 114
Richard the Lion-Hearted, 112
Roche, Otto de la, 115
Roger II, 107
Romanus II, 88, 89
Romanus III, 89, 97
Romulus Augustus, 42
Ronald of Chatillon, 109
Rumania, 123, 130
Russians, 81, 94, 95, 123

Saladin, 109, 112
Salomon, 48
Samuel, Tsar, 94-95
Santa Sophia, 94, 98, 100, 114, 130, 131
  Council of, 82
Sardica (Sofia), 19
Schism, 97-99, 108

Schlumberger, G., 87
Serbia, 120, 123, 126, 128
Serbs, 67, 94, 105, 121, 126-27, 128
Sergius, 67
Serres, 127
Severus, 7
Sicilian Vespers, 126
Sicily, 48, 72, 80, 89, 91, 106, 107, 125, 126
Sigismund, 129
Simeon, 91, 94
Sirmium (Mitrovica), 19, 41
Skeleros, Bardas, 96
Slavs, 47, 50, 63, 66, 67-68, 69, 72, 78, 85, 135
Spain, 41, 43, 47, 49, 79
Stephen II, Pope, 85
Studites, 122
Succession, system of, 6
Suidas, 100
Sun-worship, 10
Syracuse, 89
Syria, 49, 58, 70, 71, 73, 89, 90

Tamerlane, 129
Taormina, 89
Tarentum, 80, 89
Tarnikios, 101
Tarsus, 90
Thebes, 115
Themes, system of the, 71-72, 78, 90, 101
Theodat, 48
Theodora (daughter of Constantine VII), 88
Theodora (mother of Michael III), 78, 80, 83
Theodora (sister of Empress Zoë), 89, 101
Theodora, Empress, 46, 47, 58, 59, 60
Theodore, Abbot, 82
Theodore II, 116
Theodore the Studite, 84
Theodoric, 40, 42, 48
Theodosius I, 29, 30, 31, 33, 34, 35, 36, 40

Theodosius II, 30, 31, 36, 37, 38, 41
Theodosius III, 77
Theophanes, 101
Theophano, 88, 91
Theophilus, 78, 80, 82
Thessalonica, 50, 63, 68, 85, 89, 91, 94, 108, 115, 116, 127, 129
Thessaly, 68, 127
Thomas the Slav, 79, 96
Thrace, 50, 68, 69, 72, 80, 81, 94, 102, 114, 116, 119, 127, 128
Three Chapters, Council of the, 59
Tiberius, 63
Totila, King, 48
Trajan, 48
Trebizond, 115, 120, 131
Tribonian, 54
Trier, 19
Tripoli, 70
Troglita, John, 48
Turks, 127-30, 134, 135
    Seljuk, 102, 105
Tzimisces, John, 88, 89, 90, 91, 94

Ulfila, 32
Urban II, Pope, 108

Valens, 29, 40
Valentinian, 29
Valentinian III, 31
Valerius, 34
Vandals, 43, 47, 48
Varna, battle of, 130
Vasiliev, A., 50, 84
Venetians, 80, 106-7, 120, 124-25, 128
Venice, 104, 106, 107, 108, 113, 114, 119, 124-25, 127, 128, 129, 133
Vigilus, Pope, 59
Visigoths, 40-41, 42, 47, 49
Vitigus, King, 48
Vladimir, Prince, 95
Vladislav II, 130

Walter the Penniless, 108
William I, 107
William of Champlitte, 115
William of Villehardouin, 117, 123

Xiphilinus, John, 101

Zara, 113
Zealots, 122
Zeno, 30, 39, 42, 58
Zoë, Empress, 89
Zosimus, 18